Like Fire and Powder
Black Powder for the Modern Shooter

BRETT GIBBONS

Copyright © 2021 Brett A. Gibbons

All rights reserved.

ISBN: 979-8-4990-21789-4

The opinions expressed herein are those of the author, writing in a private capacity on a subject of professional military historical significance, and do not necessarily represent the position of the United States Government.

Information presented herein is provided as additional context for understanding historical processes and methods as used in the 19th century. These processes and methods are obsolete, and as 19th century technologies, they were inherently hazardous. This information should not be construed as instructions, or recommendations or guidance, for any of the processes and methods to be attempted today.

It has sometimes been urged as a reproach, that while all other military manufactures have been improved, and while every arm used in warfare has occupied the attention and exercised the inventive genius of man, gunpowder, without which the most remarkable improvements would be useless, has remained where it was. The element of truth contained in this charge is very small. If those who prefer it refer to the composition of gunpowder, then must the manufacturers plead guilty, for the proportions of the ingredients remain nearly unchanged; but if they refer to methods of preparing and purifying the ingredients, or the methods employed to produce a strong and suitable powder, we must demur.

Until lately, the manufacturer's chief aim was to produce a strong powder; then sprang up another requirement, that his powder should be clean, that is, should upon combustion leave the smallest quantity of residuum to foul the gun. In attaining cleanliness, a stronger powder was obtained; and as guns were enlarged in calibre, the charges of powder were increased till at last the problem became, how to make a gun strong enough to resist the strength of the required charge of powder. But all this has passed away, and powder is now made to suit the guns for which it is intended, instead of making guns to stand the force of the powder. Two great objects have been gained -- a diminished pressure on the gun, and an increased initial or muzzle velocity.

Gunpowder, The Westminster Review, 1870

CONTENTS

	Introduction	1
1	The Mischievous Discovery	8
2	Waltham Abbey	14
3	Saltpeter	21
4	Charcoal	33
5	Sulfur	50
6	Incorporation	52
7	Pressing	73
8	Granulation	86
9	Internal Ballistics	100
10	Final Thoughts	120

*

These violent delights have violent ends,
And in their triumph die, like fire and powder.

Shakespeare, *Romeo and Juliet*

INTRODUCTION

This is an unusual book, and of a subject and format that is very different from what I usually write. It is written for a rather narrow audience of readers: the modern black powder shooter who desires to know more about the antiquated propellant they use. As someone with a strong interest in the history of technology, I have always been fascinated by the historic processes used in producing black powder at its peak of perfection in the mid-19th century. This book also covers my experience of making my own powder, using the processes and systems from the 19th century as a guide.

I have, in fact, been making my own black powder for many years. Outside of a very close circle of friends, I have scarcely told anybody else, because their reactions are very predictable. I share my hobby and enjoyment of historical firearms with many eminent and respectable men with enviable collections of antique arms and vast domains of knowledge, but to most of them, black powder is something that is carefully dispensed from a can, which is purchased from a respectable gun shop. Only lunatics or pyromaniacs actually *make* the stuff!

Truth be told, I am probably not the sort of person you would expect to be making their own gunpowder. I don't have any particular enthusiasm for explosives and explosions, and I am a rather quiet, reserved, bookish sort of person, college educated, and I have an old dachshund. Why do I make it, then? Because I have an almost irrational obsession with recreating the original, historic performance of antique black powder rifles, and I cannot achieve this with most commercially available powders. Despite this, I still have all my fingers and eyes, and I have not blown up myself or caused any damage to property, however small. This is largely because I resist the temptation to speed up production and make large batches; an ounce or two at a time does go a little slow, and while I've never had an unexpected accident, if it was to happen, it would not result in dismemberment or worse. But make no mistake: the dragon bites, so I keep him small.

In the fall of 2021, the announced closure of the GOEX powder production by Hodgdon created great concern among muzzleloader shooters (and others) who depended largely on GOEX powder for their sporting and hunting propellant. Even before the decision to close GOEX, powder was often difficult to find, and usually expensive. Perhaps not surprisingly, many began asking questions about making their own powder. After all, black powder is 13th century technology. It is legal in most jurisdictions for most law-abiding adults to make and possess in the United States, although there are substantial laws governing the *commercial* manufacture, sale, and transportation of black powder.

In the short term there may be a (temporary) shortage of commercially-produced powder, but there is certainly no shortage of materials, books, videos, and websites covering the amateur hobbyist making black powder. There is a large pyrotechnic community that has been enthusiastically making their own black powder for decades, and although some interests overlap with the sport shooting community, we usually do not acknowledge the overlap in our interests, and view each other with some degree of suspicion. Very few people, however, are making the type of black powder that I want as a shooter of historic 19th century arms. This is a niche within a niche, but the fact remains that most people who make their own powder are making *very bad powder*. It works, almost in spite of itself. Some smoke, a bang of sorts, a bullet propelled down a barrel at unimpressive velocity, and a few hours later the maker of this substandard propellant is hammering away on Internet message boards, dispensing knowledge of how he "mastered the craft of making powder." There is a better way.

Black powder is the first manufactured energetic chemical material. From the 13th century until the first appearance of guncotton in the mid-19th century, it was all there was. Probably no other substance in modern history went through more experimentation, trial-and-error testing, and incremental improvement. Its composition has varied throughout its long history, but by the early 18th century most countries had settled on a radio equivalent to (or very close to) 75 parts potassium nitrate, 15 parts charcoal, and 10 parts of sulfur. The exact proportions varied slightly from army to army.

Black powder was still the propellant in use during the development of the modern military rifle. At the start of the 19th century, Napoleonic-style shock tactics depended largely on closing with the bayonet; battles were influenced, but not decided, by the firepower of musketry. Sixty years later, this began to change as the firepower of the rifle was revealed with incremental changes in tactics and employment in the Crimean War (1854-1856), the American Civil War (1861-1865), the Second Schleswig War (1864), the Austro-Prussian War (1866), and Franco-Prussian War (1870-1871). As early as 1859, the British Army had embraced firepower, not the bayonet, as the decisive factor on the battlefield. The Prussians followed, emphasizing firepower (*Feuertaktik*) from breechloading arms in their wars from 1864 to 1871. Black powder remained the propellant in use during the introduction of the small-bore (8mm) magazine-fed, clip-loaded bolt-action rifle. The Portuguese Kropatschek, Austro-Hungarian Mannlicher Models 1886 and 1888, and the British Lee-Metford, used black powder. By the 1890s, smokeless powder had been introduced and the armies of Europe (and eventually the United States) adopted new rifles designed to handle the higher pressures of smokeless powder, finally ending the military era of black powder.

The second half of the 19th century saw the pinnacle of black powder research and development. It was an incredibly important strategic material, upon which the survival of nations and empires depended. With the introduction of rifles, it was imperative that the black powder used be of the highest quality, producing maximum propellant gases but leaving minimal fouling residue that would build up in the rifling grooves and diminish accuracy. This motivated constant research and improvement, so that by the last decades of the 19th century, the black powder being produced for military use was the best quality powder ever made before or since. It is an unfortunate misconception, widely held among us "modern" sport shooters, that the black powder available to us today is superior to that of (for instance) the 1870s. It is not. We assume that with modern technology and processes, we can do a better job of making the stuff today than 150 years ago. Alas, the truth is quite the opposite. Except perhaps for the notable example of Swiss black powder, most modern commercially available powders would be completely unimpressive to anyone in the 1800s. It is dirtier, made with less pure ingredients, and produces a smaller volume of gas when it burns. For those curious enough to attempt making their own, it's not hard at all to make a sort of "black powder" that goes *poof* when ignited and makes a cloud of smoke and might perhaps even launch a bullet from a barrel. On the other hand, it is very hard to make anything approaching the quality, and dare I say, the *perfection*, of gunpowder from the late 1800s. This requires research and knowledge, enormous patience, a willingness to work, a stubborn refusal to cut corners, and a profoundly careful approach. But it is possible to recreate this powder today.

When shooting powder made in this way, I notice several things. Recoil is a little stronger, when compared to the same weight of modern alternatives (such as GOEX). There is noticeably less smoke. Muzzle velocities are significantly higher, even as much as 10% to 20%. There is hardly any fouling, and what fouling is encountered can be easily managed. It is just a better propellant. The reasons for this will be explained in these chapters, and in fact, is the primary purpose of this book.

There are various cheap, fast, inexpensive ways to make a kind of inferior black powder. I won't even describe them in passing. I have no interest whatsoever in wet, messy balls of goop being contaminated with dextrin and squeezed through screens. Powder made this way is perhaps barely suitable for smoothbores, or for blanks, but next to useless for rifles and in no way comparable to the excellent powders of the 19th century. In this short book, I contrast the historical process with my methods of making a *refined* product that, when perfected and consistency is achieved, will outperform commercial alternatives and give equivalent performance to those excellent powders of the 1870s.

Everything described here has been done before, historically. It is a matter of open, public record, but these were once state secrets. My purpose here is to simply describe how I make quality propellant powder, following the *spirit* if not always the *letter* of the original sources from the mid-1800s. This is what has worked for me, and that is all this is: an explanation of how I do it, which the reader may find entertaining, or perhaps useful in expanding their knowledge of just what exactly the process is (and how complex and painstaking it was) for the production of good propellant powder.

This little book is a narrative that describes how I make powder and (because I can't help myself) it is a parallel history of how powder was produced in the 19th century. The two narratives -- historical processes and how I do it -- will wind back and forth through the text. If your interest is purely in the powder, and not in the history or reasons why it was done historically a certain way, you may find this a frustrating read. I do feel it is important, especially for anyone taking a serious, and even something of a *scholarly* approach to this subject, to understand it in the historic context and to better respect and appreciate the qualities of the mid-19th century propellant that I have tried so hard to recreate.

The chymists of China or Europe had found, by casual or elaborate experiments, that a mixture of salt-petre, sulphur, and charcoal produces, with a spark of fire, a tremendous explosion. If we contrast the rapid progress of this mischievous discovery with the slow and laborious advances of reason, science, and the arts of peace, a philosopher, according to his temper, will laugh or weep at the folly of mankind.

Edward Gibbon, *The History of the Decline and Fall of the Roman Empire*

1
THIS MISCHIEVOUS DISCOVERY

In the year 2021 it may surprise you that the single largest consumer of black powder in the world is the United States military. The U.S. military requirement for black powder is some hundreds of thousands of pounds per year. The United States is also nearly unique among the nations of the world in that black powder for military use has almost always been purchased by the Government from privately-owned commercial powder mills, instead of being manufactured in military arsenals. For the first half of the United States' existence, black powder was required primarily as a *propellant* to be used in guns to fire a projectile. From Bunker Hill in 1775 to San Juan Hill in 1898, American soldiers went into battle armed with guns that used black powder to propel the bullet out of the barrel (yes, I know that the .30-40 Krag-Jorgensen was a smokeless powder rifle and was technically adopted by the U.S. Army before the Spanish American War, but there weren't enough of them and plenty of soldiers went into battle with "Trapdoor" Springfields).

Since the turn of the 20th century, however, the U.S. military's requirement for black powder has changed. It is no longer needed as a *propellant*, and is instead used for a number of applications because of the properties unique to black powder. In 2011, when I was running around Fort Benning as an officer candidate at OCS, the "arty sims" (incoming artillery and explosion simulators) our instructors used by the truckload were made mostly of black powder. So are a lot of the smokes and obscurants and other training aids, as well as saluting charges. But the most critical current-day military use of black powder is in artillery propellant charges, and the delay elements in a lot of fuze systems.

Modern artillery uses a relatively slow-burning and large-grained propellant. A small charge of black powder (from a couple ounces in light artillery to up to a pound in heavier pieces) is used as a *booster* to help ignite all of the slow-burning propellant more or less at once. Without the black powder booster, the primer would only ignite the propellant at the very end of the breech, which would progressively burn forward at a slow rate, and generate pressure very slowly. To ensure an efficient pressure curve and to propel the shell at the intended trajectory, all of the propellant needs to start burning in as little time as possible. One of the useful properties of black powder -- its very high rate of *flamespread* -- makes it particularly well suited as a booster charge that will quickly communicate flame to the entirety of the main propellant charge.

For most of the 20th century, the U.S. military obtained its black powder from the Belin Powder Works in Moosic, Pennsylvania, built by Du Pont in 1911. It was sold to GOEX in 1973, and was moved in the 1990s to the (now-closed) Army Ammunition Plant at Camp Minden, Louisiana. The manufacturing process "embraced the technology of 1850," according to a U.S. Army report from 1985. There were also a few explosions, which often caused so much damage that the Du Pont (and later GOEX) powder works were closed for extended periods. During the Cold War, the U.S. Army was reasonably concerned that a catastrophic accident at the GOEX plant could deprive the military of a strategic material, and the Army built its own backup black powder plant in Charlestown, Indiana, which opened in 1978, but has since been entirely decommissioned. The black powder produced for military use is made to a military specification, "MIL-P-223B POWDER, BLACK," which itself was made from milspec charcoal, "JAN-C-178 CHARCOAL (For Use in Munitions)." The black powder milspec requires a specific gravity (density) that "shall not exceed the limits of 1.72 minimum and 1.80 max for glazed powder." It is not a coincidence that the Material Safety Data Sheet for GOEX black powder, in 2021, states a density between 1.72 and 1.80, because it is made to milspec MIL-P-223B and still used for military applications.

It is important to remember that *none* of the black powder produced to U.S. military specifications is *intended* for use as a propellant for firearms. Instead, it is intended for other applications, such as fuzes, primers, igniters, and booster charges, etc. The U.S. military does not care how much residue (fouling) is left behind when this black powder burns, nor does the U.S. military care how much propellant gas is produced when the powder burns. All the military cares about is *consistency* between lots, and measurable, predictable burning and flamespread rates. You may be astonished to learn that GOEX black powder, which you may have been using for your whole life, isn't even made as a propellant for firearms. It *works* in firearms, but it's made to a milspec for other applications.

If you're reading this, it's probably safe to assume that your interest in black powder is as a *propellant* to push a projectile out of the barrel of a black powder firearm. So, as black powder shooters, the properties of black powder that *we* want are different from the properties of black powder that the modern-day United States armed forces want. For propellant powder, we desire three things. First, we want the greatest possible volume of propellant gases to be generated by the combustion of the powder. Second, we want the least possible amount of combustion byproducts (fouling) to be left behind when the powder burns. Third, we want the true burn rate of the powder (which is determined by its density) to be within the ideal window for maximum performance in firearms. Unfortunately for us, the military no longer requires any of these desirable aspects of black powder for current-day use. As long as the flamespread and burn rates are consistent for military purposes, the black powder used by the military can generate pitiful quantities of gas, and leave behind all kinds of fouling residue. None of that matters, because it's either being blown to shards as part of a fuze assembly, or being blown out the muzzle of a 105mm howitzer.

As I've already mentioned in the introduction, the black powder produced in the late 19th century, when black powder was still being produced and used primarily as a *propellant*, was the best ever made. It was amazing stuff, producing a large volume of propellant gases and leaving behind very little fouling residue. Every step of the production process, and every aspect of the preparation and purity of the ingredients, was focused on making the best possible gunpowder for use in firearms. This was the result of several centuries of constant experimentation and incremental improvement.

Before proceeding, it may be useful to define some common terms and basic facts about gunpowder. The composition usually cited is the Anglo-American proportion of 75 parts saltpeter, 15 parts charcoal, and 10 parts sulfur. These were the preferred ratios of the three components in British and American gunpowder, throughout the 19th century. They were not, however, the universally adopted compositions. On the Continent, there were considerable variations in the ratios of the ingredients. It is fair to say that the Anglo-American composition of 75-15-10 has stood the test of time, and has been proven to produce some of the best powder ever made. William Greener, a British gunsmith and author of several influential books on gunnery, observed in 1858 that British gunpowder was recognized as the best in Europe, even by the French, who were usually considered superior chemists. "It is rather singular," Greener remarked, "that we should excel those who pride themselves so much on their chemical knowledge; but, as before remarked, it is certain that the intimate incorporation of the ingredients is of more importance than the chemical proportions." He was certainly correct, in that the processes of manufacture and incorporation of the ingredients was more important than the exact ratios of ingredients used.

Proportions of Ingredients.

		Saltpetre.	Charcoal.	Sulphur.
	By the atomic theory............	74.64	13.51	11.85
IN THE UNITED STATES:				
	For the military service.......	76	14	10
		75	15	10
	For sporting.......................	78	12	10
		77	13	10
IN ENGLAND:	For the military service......	75	15	10
	For sporting.......................	78	14	8
		75	17	8
IN FRANCE:	For the military service......	75	12.5	12.5
	For sporting.......................	78	12	10
	For blasting.......................	62	18	20
IN PRUSSIA:	For the military service......	75	13.5	11.5
IN SPAIN:	For the military service......	76.5	12.7	10.8

Black powder is usually found (both historically and today) in the form of a coarse powder of grains, more or less the consistency of average sand, or a little smaller. Several systems of measurement have been adopted for sorting black powder by the size of the grains. One system sorts the powder into seven distinct classes, with Class 1 being the largest, and Class 7 the smallest. The U.S. Ordnance Manual in the 1860s set forth the seven classes of gunpowder, and this system has endured; the U.S. military still uses the class designations for black powder to this day. Sporting powder is classified by fineness of grain with a convention that is probably familiar to most readers, using the letter F to designate powder for sporting arms. The letter F is commonly given a suffix of a lower case *g*, which indicates the powder has been *glazed*. We will cover glazing extensively in a later chapter, but for now, *glazed* powder means it has been tumbled to polish the grains and free them from any dust. A powder indicated as Fg represents a *fine grain glazed powder*. It corresponds to about a Class 3 sized powder, which is suitable for large-bore rifles and muskets, of at least .50-caliber. Adding another F to the indication means the powder is an even smaller grain: an FFg powder is approximately Class 4, and is often used in many of the Civil War-era rifle-muskets and some .45 to .50-caliber rifles. FFFg is about a Class 6, and is still used in some rifles when shooting charges significantly reduced from the military "service" charge, and in black powder pistols. Class 7 powder is FFFFg, too fine for use as a propellant powder for most applications, but is most commonly encountered for flintlock priming.

The superior quality universally attributed to the English powders is attested by the results of my experiments with them. I would, therefore, propose the Waltham powder as the type or standard to which our powder for military service should comfort in nearly all respects.

Major Alfred Mordecai, U.S. Army Ordnance Department, 1848

2
WALTHAM ABBEY

I attempt to follow, as closely as possible, the written description of gunpowder manufacture as it was carried out by the British Government's Royal Gunpowder Mills at Waltham Abbey. This factory produced gunpowder for the small arms and artillery of the British Army and Royal Artillery, and in 1870, required a work force of 150 men. Most of the processes were automated, and the workers were principally employed in the loading of the raw materials and movement of the materials between stages in the manufacturing process. Major Baddeley wrote a description of the process in 1859, Captain Goodenough added further notes after collaboration with Colonel Boxer of the Royal Laboratory in 1868, and Captain F. M. Smith published an updated description in 1870. The only significant change in these 11 years was a modification primarily of the density of the small arms powder used, to perform better in the Martini-Henry rifle then under development.

I am, admittedly, an Anglophile, but my reasons for following the Waltham Abbey methods are also practical. The U.S. military never had a Government-owned black powder factory during the 19th century. Even in 1862, as the Civil War was reaching its peak of violence, the U.S. Army Ordnance Manual casually mentions that "Gunpowder for the military service is made by private contractors." This tradition of the U.S. military buying powder from commercial powder-makers is older than the United States itself. In 1775, when King George III suspended gunpowder deliveries from England to the American colonies, the Frankford Powder Mill near Philadelphia, Pennsylvania became the sole source of American gunpowder. The Continental Congress contracted with Frankford in January 1776, and the U.S. military would buy its black powder from private sources ever since, except for a very brief period in the late 1970s (yes, 1970s, Jimmy Carter, bell-bottom pants, big hair, Cold War) into the 1980s, when a small portion of the U.S. military's requirement for black powder was produced at a Government mill in Indiana. This means there is ample literature from British Government sources on the production of black powder at Waltham Abbey, and next to nothing on the production of powder from private American powder mills.

English powder was also understood to be *the best*. Again in 1862, the U.S. Ordnance Manual did not hesitate to say that "English gunpowder – particularly their sporting-powder – has long been noted for its excellence, which is due to the care taken in selecting the best materials, and the skill in combining them." Perhaps the highest compliment came from the French, who purchased their fine sporting powder (*poudre de chasse*) from commercial English sources for much of the 19th century. The availability of good primary documentation on the production of English powder, and the excellent reputation of this powder as being truly among the best ever made, has made Waltham Abbey powder the ideal form that I seek to replicate.

In some situations, I am unable to exactly follow the Waltham Abbey methods. Most of these situations are because I simply do not have a massive powder mill with all of the dedicated machinery used in the process. What I use, however, is a close approximation and reasonable modern substitute for the Victorian methods that follow documented procedures carried out in the 19th century in the powder mills of Europe. The end result is essentially the same: a supremely high quality powder.

Black powder is the intimate mix of three ingredients: charcoal, sulfur, and potassium nitrate. When ignited, it burns and produces a volume of hot gases that is many times greater than its volume as a solid. The majority of the products of combustion are solids, and in a gun most of them are blown out the muzzle but a quantity will inevitably remain in the barrel as a *fouling*. What I sought to produce, and what they produced at Waltham Abbey, is a propellant that creates the greatest possible volume of propellant gas, while leaving the least possible fouling. It is also of obvious importance that the powder be as consistent as possible; it is no good to have one batch produce starkly different ballistic results than another batch. With care and attention, it is possible to achieve all of these objectives.

Making powder is a scientific art. While much of the process is mere chemistry, because it involves organic and inorganic materials, there is more to it than mixing the component ingredients together and running it through a press. Some things cannot be known, without expensive and delicate laboratory facilities. How much ash is in the charcoal? How long should the components be incorporated? There is no gauge or chart or device that can tell you this. It comes of experience. In time, with experience, I came to know what was correct by sight, smell, and touch. Sometimes improvements were accidental, and a batch of powder I expected to be mediocre turned out to perform much better.

I've been a rifle shooter since my teens. Although I have enjoyed shooting everything from military-issued medium machine guns to modern commercial semi-automatics, I am always drawn back to my favorite rifle, the Pattern 1853 Enfield rifle-musket. This is the rifle I spend the most time with, and I enjoy stretching its legs out to "long" distances up to 600 yards. The sights on the rifle go up to 900, but as a practical matter, the .577 bore, slow twist, and relatively low velocity make consistent shooting beyond 600 yards something of a fleeting challenge. My targets are steel, and generous in size: 4 feet square. Set up out in the open desert of the American southwest, on a still, chilly morning, my P/53 Enfields will sling lead into steel, and two or three seconds later, reward me with an immensely satisfying *claaaang* echoing back from the target. I shoot the rifles in their military configuration -- no aftermarket custom sights, no special trigger work -- and with ammunition that precisely matches the original historic military cartridge, which has been the pursuit of practically my entire adult life. Others find this incredibly boring, and they usually don't hesitate to tell me so. The P/53 is not an extremely accurate rifle, by modern standards of judgment (especially in its conventional infantry configuration). It's a muzzleloader. It's absurdly long in the eyes and hands of people accustomed to modern sporting carbines, and you can't use it in a 3-gun competition (well, you could, I guess... that actually might be fun to try). But I find a perfect joy in shooting my P/53's and achieving precisely the same results, in ballistic performance and accuracy of shooting, as recorded and documented by the British Army in the 1850s and 1860s. It is an intersection of so many of my interests: shooting guns, historical research, and an analysis and appreciation for the profound paradigm-shifting changes that the P/53 (and its contemporaries) wrought in battlefield tactics and the role, status, and training of the individual soldier.

Before I seriously began looking deeper into the history and context of those revolutionary first-generation rifled weapons, I assumed (probably like most black powder shooters) that pretty much all black powder was the same. GOEX, Elephant, Diamondback, KIK, Schuetzen, Swiss... they were all just mixtures of the same three ingredients, and pretty much the same since the 1400s. Swiss powder, it was rumored, did not foul as much as the others, but nobody could really tell me why. I bought whatever was cheapest. As my interests grew to be more serious, I learned that all black powders were not the same, and then came the painful realization that the gunpowder they had in the 1860s was unquestionably better than the stuff we are shooting today. This is what prompted me to consider making my own, not because it was cheaper, and not because commercial black powder was not available (in relative abundance), but because I wanted something better, which could approach the propellant gunpowders that were historically used in the P/53. Today, many years later, a pandemic and other contributing factors have resulted in a shortage of commercially produced black powder, along with pretty much everything else related to the shooting sports. Interest in making black powder is probably at an all-time high.

The gunpowder used by the Pattern 1853 Enfield was purposefully developed to achieve maximum performance in that rifle. For the first few years, from 1854 to 1859, the P/53 used the legacy small arms "Fine Grain" or F.G. powder, so-named to distinguish it from the Large Grain or

L.G. powder, that was used for cannon. It was the same stuff, made by exactly the same processes using willow or alder charcoal and as the names suggest, the only difference was the size of the grains it was broken up into. The assistant superintendent of the Waltham Abbey gunpowder mill recalled that, "On the introduction of rifled small arms, F.G. was found unsuitable. This necessitated the entire separation of the manufacture of small arm powder from that of powder for guns." Extensive experiments were conducted, and in 1859 a new gunpowder using only alder buckthorn (dogwood) charcoal known as "Enfield Rifle" or E.R. was adopted. It had a larger grain size than the old F.G. powder, and after a year of widespread practical use, the size of the grain was increased yet again in 1860 to the final form. The grains would pass through a mesh with 12 holes per inch, but not pass through a mess with 20 holes per inch. This 12 to 20 mesh powder was still often called E.R. powder but formally known as "J.2" until it was renamed "Rifle Fine Grain" or R.F.G. in 1865. There's nothing like R.F.G. available today. It was a large grained powder (we would call it Fg or "one-F" powder in modern terms) but it was also made to a fairly low density of 1.55 grams per cubic centimeter. A lower density powder truly burns faster than a higher density powder, but this was contrasted with the larger grain size which had less surface area compared to smaller grain powders, and therefore took longer time to burn. These unique characteristics were developed purposefully for the Pattern 1853 rifle and its "perfected" ammunition, a .550-inch bullet with wooden plug, recommended by Captain Boxer of the Royal Laboratory at Woolwich arsenal, in 1859. In 1876, an officer at the Royal Gunpowder Factory at Waltham Abbey observed "And now, as far as we know, no powder excels R.F.G. in shooting qualities in the Enfield rifle."

    I have obsessively sought to recreate R.F.G. powder, in order to shoot the P/53 Enfield rifle with the most historically accurate propellant and projectile. After many years, I have been successful and my version of R.F.G. gives me very satisfactory results. Of course, my ridiculous obsession with precisely recreating R.F.G. has only been a personal challenge and a hobby, and perfectly good gunpowder that gives good, consistent results can be made with far less painstaking effort at matching the properties and performance of a specific historic powder.

Making my own powder has also given me an enormously expanded appreciation for black powder, its role as a propellant, and how the smallest and seemingly insignificant differences can dramatically affect its performance. The process is challenging, but can be very fun, and I sincerely believe it can be done in perfect safety, as long as basic common sense precautions are taken. Amateur pyrotechnics have been making their own powder for generations, but the black powder shooting sport has only recently seemed to warm up to the idea of homemade propellant. When I first started, only about a decade ago, I was almost embarrassed to mention to other shooters that I was making my own powder. "You'll blow yourself up!" they said. Today, many of the same people who rolled their eyes at the idea of making powder a few years ago are now asking me about it, if only as a short-term option until commercially produced powder is available again. In fact, I fall into this same category: I've made my own black powder, and it's excellent stuff that meets all my needs, but I also appreciate Swiss black powder and use quite a bit of it, especially when my schedule is tight and I don't have the luxury of time to spend making my own.

> And that it was great pity, so it was,
> This villainous saltpeter should be digged
> Out of the bowels of the harmless earth,
> Which many a good tall fellow had destroyed
> So cowardly; and but for these vile guns,
> He would himself have been a soldier.
>
> Shakespeare, *Henry IV*

3
SALTPETER

Known historically (and still commonly today) as *saltpeter*, a molecule of potassium nitrate consists of an atom of potassium, another of nitrogen, and three of oxygen. We need it for the oxygen; the potassium and nitrogen come along for the ride and contribute to the useless byproducts of combustion (fouling). Propellant powders can be made from other forms of nitrates, but potassium nitrate has been consistently the best, and easiest and safest to work with. In the presence of a significant proportion of potassium nitrate, which provides an abundance of oxygen, charcoal burns with powerful rapidity. This is all black powder is: charcoal burning really fast.

Potassium nitrate is not toxic unless consumed or inhaled in absurdly large concentrations; in fact, small quantities are used as the active ingredient in toothpaste for people with sensitive teeth. It is also a common curing salt for meats, especially things like corned beef and salami. There are many other common industrial and artistic uses.

For *good* powder, it is essential for the potassium nitrate to be as pure as possible. Historically, Waltham Abbey received its saltpeter from India in an impure state known as *grough* (pronounced like gruff). The grough saltpeter was 97% pure, and enormous effort was put into purifying the nitrate to very nearly 100%. Can powder be made with 97% pure potassium nitrate? Yes, but it will not be *good* or *consistent* powder. If the powder is to be used as a propellant in guns, and not for fireworks or rocket motors, there is absolutely no reason to even bother making the stuff with impure potassium nitrate. If there are impurities in the saltpeter, the impurities are very likely to end up deposited inside your gun barrel as fouling. This is the reason why the British (and every other country producing gunpowder for military use) went to enormous pains to obtain extremely pure potassium nitrate. Most of the popular "Internet message board" sources of potassium nitrate, such as stump remover, are completely unsuitable in their unpurified states even if, as they are often touted, "almost pure." Black powder made with impure saltpeter will never be the ballistic equivalent of any commercial powders, and at best, it will cause an unusually rapid accumulation of fouling.

How pure does it need to be? At Waltham Abbey, it was made pure enough that other organic or inorganic substances were not detectable in it with simple litmus tests. It was probably in excess of 99.8% pure.

Unfortunately, very pure (99.5% or better) potassium nitrate suitable for making propellant powder is expensive, and found online from $5 to $10 a pound (or more) in the United States, and that is usually before shipping costs. Buying it pure will save time, and a lot of work. However, I've found that the purity cannot be guaranteed, and will vary. I can almost guarantee that "pure" potassium nitrate purchased online, especially from anyone marketing to the amateur fireworks consumer, is not actually going to be pure enough for quality propellant gunpowder. It may cross the threshold of "good enough," but I do not go to the trouble of making my own gunpowder to simply be good enough.

It is necessary, in most circumstances, to purify the potassium nitrate.

The cheapest potassium nitrate is fertilizer grade. It can often be found for well under $2 a pound and is usually around 95% to 97% pure, comparable to the grough saltpeter at Waltham Abbey. Sometimes it is *prilled,* or formed into little balls for easy pouring; I avoid the prilled nitrate whenever possible because it usually contains a binding substance (it is also usually more expensive).

Saltpeter has a remarkable quality that makes it fairly simple and efficient to purify: the amount that can be dissolved in water increases dramatically as the temperature of the water rises. Hot, boiling water can hold an incredible amount of saltpeter dissolved in solution, but cold near-freezing water will hardly keep any. Meanwhile, most of the impurities that are found in grough saltpeter will dissolve readily into cold water, and stay dissolved. "Hence," Captain Smith explains, "if a boiling saturated solution of the [grough saltpeter] be made and allowed to cool, it will deposit the excess of saltpeter, and retain the other salts in solution." As the temperature of the solution cools, the water cannot hold all the saltpeter dissolved in it, and the pure potassium nitrate will *precipitate* in the form of fine, white little crystals, while the impurities remain dissolved in the water. To describe this formally, water at 212° Fahrenheit will hold 39 parts of sodium chloride (table salt) and 240 parts of potassium nitrate; at 70° Fahrenheit, the water will still hold 36 parts of sodium chloride, but only 32 parts of potassium nitrate. The other 208 parts of potassium nitrate would precipitate out as pure crystals, with a trace 3-part amount of sodium chloride crystals.

Hot water will hold an astonishing, almost unbelievable amount of potassium nitrate dissolved in solution, up to two and a half times the weight of the water. At Waltham Abbey, when preparing a new batch for purification, 270 imperial gallons of water was mixed with two imperial tons of grough saltpeter. Consider that an imperial gallon is somewhat more than a U.S. gallon, and an imperial ton is 2240 pounds instead of the short ton (2000 pounds) commonly used in the U.S. This proportion by weight was roughly 1.66 parts of saltpeter to 1 part of water, at ordinary cool temperature, although even at Waltham Abbey, these were general guidelines and the grough saltpeter was not weighed to any degree of precision, and neither was the water measured with much precision. There was probably a deviation of 5% either way. If you want this in metric measurements, then you should have won the damn war.

Just kidding. 270 imperial gallons, and two imperial tons, works out to 1227 liters of water and 2032 kilograms of nitrate. The ratio is still the same: 1.66 kilograms of nitrate to every liter of water. This is nowhere close to the maximum amount of potassium nitrate that can theoretically be dissolved into water: at 100 degrees Celsius, 2.5 kilograms of saltpeter will dissolve into one liter of water.

At Waltham Abbey, distilled water was preferred for this process (yes, they were *that* concerned about impurities, when making gunpowder in the 1870s). "Distilled water should, if possible, be alone employed," Captain Smith cautioned. "At Waltham Abbey the water used is from an artesian well, and is remarkably free from mineral impurities." Unfortunately, I live in an area with extremely hard water, in fact some of the hardest water found in the continental United States, and therefore I buy distilled water. But because distilled water is sold by the

U.S. gallon in these United States, I have to convert back to U.S. standard units. For one gallon of distilled water, I add 13 pounds of potassium nitrate. A little more, or a little less, will do no harm. I use a very large boiling pot that comfortably holds several gallons.

Water and nitrate go into the pot, and the solution is brought to a boil. In the proportion of 1.66 parts nitrate to 1 part water, it will reach boiling at a temperature rather significantly higher than the ordinary boiling point of water. This is a heavily saturated solution at temperatures above that of boiling water, and if it splashes on anyone, it causes much more serious burns. Depending on the starting purity of the nitrate, scummy residue may rise to the top, especially if the nitrate came in prilled form. The enormous copper vat holding hundreds of gallons of water and two imperial tons of saltpeter dissolved in solution at Waltham Abbey was kept boiling for 30 minutes, while any scum was raked off the surface. At this point, a little cold water was dashed onto the surface, which would help cause some impurities to crystallize and fall to the bottom. If there's no scum rising, there is no particular reason to boil the solution for any longer than a couple minutes. Longer or shorter boiling time will make no difference on the final product.

The solution of water, potassium nitrate, and also all the dissolved impurities, was known in 19th century refining vernacular as the *mother liquor*. Because the mixture is only 1.6kg of nitrate for every liter of water, well below the maximum amount of up to 2.5kg per liter that boiling water could hold in solution, even as the solution begins to cool down, it will not start to precipitate crystals right away. This is done deliberately and allows for a few minutes "working time" for filtering before it cools to the point that crystallization begins to occur.

At Waltham Abbey, a hose was lowered into the cauldron with the solution, and a hand pump was used to pulp the solution into a trough. The solution flowed down the trough and into several holes, each hole leading to a pipe pointing straight down. A special type of "filtering bag" was attached to each pipe, and the solution ran into the bags. The water was still quite hot enough that it could easily hold the potassium nitrate dissolved in solution, but any other substances and impurities that were not dissolved in the water were filtered out. The bags were made of *dowlas*, a strong coarse linen cloth used for things like soldier's gaiters, aprons, and pockets for 19th century working men's trousers. Today it still has a niche use, as part of the ecclesiastical garments for clergy, and it costs $40 a yard. In 1870 dowlas was a cheap, tough fabric that stood up well to hard work, but it is not strictly necessary that saltpeter solution be filtered by dowlas. Any cheap basic linen cloth will work, and cheaper is actually better in this case, because the expensive (high thread count) linens are too tightly woven.

In my first attempts, years ago, I filtered my solution using coffee filters. What an awful, messy, painstaking, time-consuming nightmare! The coffee filters got the crud out of the solution, but being very small, and intended for only a coffee-cup volume of fluid, they quickly stopped working, fell apart, and were generally unworkable.

A piece of fairly coarse linen cloth tied loosely over a large pot or pail works perfectly. The solution is still extremely hot; I avoid plastic tubs or buckets and use another large kitchen pot to receive the filtered solution beneath the linen cloth. If the filtering is taking too long, I will put the pot up to simmer on the stove, to warm the water back up to near-boiling and prevent the saltpeter from crystallizing too soon. When using prilled potassium nitrate fertilizer, the clay-like binder substance can quickly clog the filter cloth, and it may be necessary to use several cloths. Usually, however, filtering goes quite fast. The solution that passes through the filter cloth is normally a little clearer, and free of foreign solid objects like sand. It is very important to ensure there are no foreign objects in the nitrate (or any of the other ingredients) as they may be a spark-causing hazard later in the production process.

As the solution cools, potassium nitrate will begin to precipitate as crystals. When I first started purifying my nitrate, I would let the pot sit until it was very cool, and then recover the crystals, on the assumption that these crystals were pure. The crystals were in fact pure, but they were very large, and when allowed to form large crystals, they trapped pockets of the mother liquor (which still contains dissolved impurities) in them. These large crystals were definitely purer than what I started with, and made reasonably good powder, but the Waltham Abbey process adds a simple step to prevent the mother liquor being trapped inside the crystals. "If the solution were left to crystallize without agitation the salt would be deposited in the form of large crystals, each of which would enclose a small quantity of this impure mother liquor. To prevent this the liquor in the coolers must be kept in constant agitation, to cause it to deposit the salt in the form of 'flour' or minute crystals."

The solution was run into a long, shallow trough that was constantly stirred by a worker with a wooden implement. As the temperature dropped, the nitrate fell out of the solution in the form of tiny crystals and the stirring kept them from forming larger crystals trapping solution inside. These small crystals were moved over to one side of the trough as they accumulated, where it was shoveled out with a copper shovel. The crystals were placed on an inclined board that allowed any excess water to drain back into the trough.

I use a large galvanized tub that would probably hold ten gallons as my "cooling trough." This critical piece of gunpowder making infrastructure was found while visiting my mother's house for Easter a couple years ago. The tub owes me some gratitude, since my mother had doomed it to the ignominious fate of being a decorative flowerbed in the garden. Quietly, when she was off on some errand, I got it into my pickup truck, and saved it from a dubious agricultural legacy. I have repurposed the tub to serve a noble and honorable purpose as a cooling trough for gunpowder making. Its disappearance was blamed on mischievous neighborhood rascals who probably wanted it for making drugs or something.

The solution goes into the tub at 190° Fahrenheit. No crystal should precipitate at this temperature. For making some of my first batches of purified nitrate many years ago, I would put a smaller plastic container with the hot solution on an empty shelf in the freezer (incidentally also my mother's freezer, at the time, but what she doesn't know won't hurt anybody). While I thought this would quickly cool the solution and cause the saltpeter to precipitate out in less time (which indeed it did), it was counterproductive as the rapid cooling caused precipitation too quickly, forming the impure and undesirable large crystals. It is best to be patient, put on some music or a podcast, and watch the solution as it cools for the first sign of crystals forming. They will look a bit like snowflakes, forming first on the surface, but gently stirring the solution will cause them to sink to the bottom. As they accumulate, I use a flat-ended wooden spatula (you can usually find these conveniently located in the kitchen drawers) to scrape the crystals over to the side, and once I have a little pile of them, I scoop them out, letting as much of the water drain off of them as possible.

Here I deviate slightly from Waltham Abbey's procedures, although in the future I may change this. I have not placed the crystals on an inclined board to let excess solution run back into the tub. Instead I place the crystals on a sheet of aluminum foil next to the sink, and allow the excess solution to seep off of them into the sink.

There is still saltpeter in the lost solution, but it is a relatively small amount. Waltham Abbey saved this solution that drained from the crystals to maximize production efficiency and save costs. Losing a few pennies worth of saltpeter down the drain does not bother me too much, although I admit, it would be too easy to place the crystals on a board and let it drain back into the tub.

For maximum purity of crystals, once the solution drops below 90° Fahrenheit, I stop scooping out the crystals. At this temperature, the rate of precipitation has slowed considerably. In fact it was so slow, that Waltham Abbey found it was no longer worth the cost of paying a worker to stir the solution and scoop out the crystals with the copper shovel after it fell below 90°. Also, below this temperature the precipitating crystal starts to contain more impurities from the mother liquor, or at least this was the belief at Waltham Abbey. About 75% of the saltpeter in the solution precipitates out during the temperature drop from 190° to 90°. If the potassium nitrate was 97% pure to start with, at this point the solution is likely to contain 77.4% potassium nitrate while 22.6% of the other materials dissolved in the solution are impurities (almost certainly a preponderance of sodium chloride, which is table salt, and some sodium sulphate).

Briefly forgetting the little snowy mound of white crystals that has been yielded from the solution, the question remains, what to do with the remaining solution? Since the remaining solution contains about 25% of the total amount of potassium nitrate that we started with, it is certainly worth saving. It cannot be purified any further on its own without complicated laboratory equipment. All that can be done is to evaporate off the water, collect up the crystals that are left (which are mostly saltpeter but thoroughly contaminated with impurities), and save them for the next batch. Just as was done at Waltham Abbey, I pour the remaining mother liquor into a pan in anticipation of evaporating off the moisture (more excess liquid containing recoverable saltpeter can also be added to this after the next steps).

Back to the little mound of snowy crystals, the fruit of all this labor. The crystals are very nearly pure saltpeter but they are still wet with the mother liquor and the impurities dissolved in it. The crystals must be *washed* to remove the mother liquor still coating the crystals, and for this process, distilled water again is preferred. Sometimes I follow the Waltham Abbey method of giving the crystals three washings, and sometimes I only do the first washing. Whether it's one washing or three, it is most important that the crystals get washed right after they have finished draining. I do not want the water in the mother liquor evaporating and leaving impurities coating the crystals. A fine-holed colander works well for the first washing, and like the Waltham Abbey process, water is simply poured through the crystals and allowed to drain out through the colander. At Waltham Abbey they saved this water, because it does contain a small amount of recoverable nitrate.

For the first washing, I slowly drizzle a half gallon of very cold distilled water over the crystals in the colander. I try to use water as close to freezing as possible. The object is to wash off the exterior of the crystals, and the colder the water is, the less potassium nitrate will be dissolved into it. Simply running a little water over the crystals will remove most of the contaminates, but at Waltham Abbey the nitrate was subjected to two more washings. After the first rinse, the crystals were completely immersed in cold water for thirty minutes, and the water was then allowed to drain out by removing a plug at the bottom of the basin. The nitrate was allowed to drain for another thirty minutes. Finally, more cold water was run over the crystals like the first washing. Having been washed three times, the nitrate was now considered essentially pure and suitable for gunpowder. There is certainly no harm in doing all three washings; perhaps it is just laziness on my part that I usually only rinse the crystals once, but given the much smaller size of my batches, I think my single rinse probably removes more of the contaminants than the first washing of the very large quantity of crystals at Waltham Abbey.

A final note on the washings: the water used to rinse and wash the crystals will contain a small amount of dissolved potassium nitrate. If the water is simply disposed of, this amount will be lost. I let this water run down the drain, but at Waltham Abbey it was all collected and saved. The water from the first washing was added to what remained of the mother liquor, and water from the second and third washing (containing mostly pure saltpeter with trace contaminants) was saved to be put back into the first large boiling pot with the next batch of grough saltpeter. As for the mother liquor, it went into another pot and was boiled until half the water was boiled off, then poured through another set of filters, and allowed to crystallize. These crystals were about 50% saltpeter, and the remaining salts were impurities. They were gathered up when dry and would be put back into the large boiling pot along with the next load of grough saltpeter. In this way, there was very little loss of any saltpeter. When dealing with tons of saltpeter at a time, recovering the nitrate from the residual mother liquor and water from the washings represented enough savings to be worth the labor. For my purposes, perhaps a dollar or two worth of potassium nitrate in the leftover mother liquor is not worth the hour of extra work.

Once washed and drained, the crystals are ready to be turned into gunpowder. They should be fairly well drained, although the potassium nitrate does not have to be bone-dry. At first, I would dry the crystals completely by putting them in the oven at low temperature for a time, but found that this caused them to stick aggressively to the baking pan that I had liberated from its ignominious prior occupation as an implement my mother used for cookie-making. I still prefer the crystals mostly dry, but a small amount of moisture of 3% to 5% of the weight is perfectly acceptable, and this was actually preferred at Waltham Abbey, where it was declared "the saltpeter used for powder-making should always be used moist."

If the crystals must be stored, they should be well dried. I have stored purified potassium nitrate crystals in heavy "ziplock" freezer bags for years with no perceptible harm.

4
CHARCOAL

More so than any other factor, the charcoal determines the quality and performance of the powder. It is supremely important. Everything else can be done perfectly, the other components purified to the maximum possible extent, and the powder will fail if the charcoal is no good. The species of wood used to make the charcoal, and the physical techniques and procedures in its production, are absolutely crucial. To make truly excellent powder with all the qualities of good 19th century gunpowder, a consistent and high quality charcoal is essential.

The charcoal is also the hardest component to consistently achieve. It is in the making of the charcoal that the production of powder most closely resembles an art, rather than a science. Countless volumes have been written on the production of gunpowder over the last several hundred years, and the enigmatic question of the charcoal has never been completely answered. Because black powder is still used significantly in various components of military ordnance to this day, research into the methods of production of charcoal, and its other qualities, are still being carried out. There is a lot that we still really just don't know, even with the help of powerful microscopes and the most advanced laboratory equipment in the world.

It is not too much of an exaggeration to say that gunpowder *is* charcoal. The charcoal is the fuel: the potassium nitrate merely provides the oxygen so that it can rapidly burn in the absence of atmospheric oxygen. The particles of potassium nitrate, intimately mixed with the charcoal, allow the charcoal to burn in a very fast yet progressive state, and produce considerably greater heat. Sulfur, too, adds to this reaction, as we will cover shortly. But charcoal is the key component, and mastering the consistently repeatable production of good charcoal is probably the single most important aspect of the whole process.

Charcoal begins, obviously, as wood grown by a living tree or shrub, and as such it is an organic matter containing fiber, moisture, oils, etc. Hundreds of years of powder making have revealed that certain species of trees and shrubs produce intrinsically better charcoal for propellant gunpowder than other species. When I first started making powder, many years ago, I made my first batches of charcoal using wood from the ubiquitous pepper tree that grows profusely in the semi-arid environment of Southern California's coast. It worked, to a degree, and I was able to make a powder that was "good" by most general standards, but not remotely comparable to the superior powders of the 19th century. Gunpowder can be made with charcoal from just about any plant, and even from plywood, but it will certainly not be *good* powder. The first important part of the charcoal-making process, and the part over which there is the most control, is selecting what species of wood to use.

Different woods have different qualities, some more or less desirable in gunpowder. For instance, some woods are known to produce a powder that is very powerful (i.e. produces a greater volume of propellant gas), but is less consistent and can cause variations between batches. Such a powder would give high muzzle velocities, but the velocities might vary between batches, resulting in different points of impact from the same gun, with the same load and bullet. Other woods are known to produce a less powerful gunpowder but are far more consistent. Cost of the wood, and rate of growth of the plant, are also important factors.

By the early 19th century, the ideal woods for gunpowder charcoal had been identified after extensive experimentation and study. These remain the common woods for gunpowder production to this day. There are four usual species encountered: willow, alder, maple, and the alder buckthorn. Willow and alder were preferred for large-grain powders for artillery and mortars, while the alder buckthorn was exclusively used at Waltham Abbey for small arms powder. In the United States, willow and maple were commonly used, and until very recently the common GOEX black powder was made with maple charcoal.

In the 19th century, alder buckthorn was commonly known to charcoal makers as "dogwood" although it was recognized that this was technically not accurate, and identified as *Rhamnus frangula* by the famed botanist Carl Linnaeus. It is sometimes called "berry-bearing alder" due to the large bunches of toxic berries it grows. Genetic testing in the 20th century reclassified it as *Frangula alnus,* and today we know that alder buckthorn isn't really an alder at all and the plant never had thorns.

Gunpowder made from alder buckthorn (Dogwood) was found to produce as much as 10% more propellant gas than gunpowders made from other woods. This made it highly prized for making powder for military rifles, due to the considerably higher velocities that alder buckthorn charcoal could impart to the bullet. Around 1860, the velocity of the British Army's general issue Pattern 1853 Enfield rifle-musket was accurately measured to be 1260 feet per second, and this relatively high velocity (by 1860 standards) resulted in a longer *dangerous space*, which is the distance of ground over which a bullet fired at a certain range can be expected to hit a 6-foot tall target. The longer the *dangerous space*, the more effective a rifle is on the battlefield.

Alder buckthorn is native to nearly all of Europe and

	Proportions of Gas. Cubic inches.
Dogwood (*Rhamnus frangula*)	80–84
Willow (*Salix alba*)	76–78
Alder	74–73
Filbert	72
Fir, Chesnut, Hazel	66
Elm	62
Oak	61–63
Mahogany	58
Willow (*overheated*)	59–66
Oak	54–56

Comparative volumes of propellant gas produced by equal charges of gunpowder made with various species of wood. The "dogwood" or alder buckthorn produces the most gas, by a large margin.

grows as far west as China. It is commonly used as a shrub for hedges. In the United States and Canada, it was introduced in the 19th century and has become an invasive species. Several states (such as Connecticut) have made deliberate efforts to eradicate it. My powder has never used alder buckthorn, because I live in the western United States and it will not grow here. Because it is an invasive species, it is controlled and cannot be purchased online or brought into other states. So for all the excellent properties of alder buckthorn, and its use at Waltham Abbey to make excellent propellant powder, I haven't been able to use it. Here again, I must deviate from the Waltham Abbey process out of necessity.

Through a fortunate bit of cosmic luck, I do happen to live in the relatively small part of the world where pacific willow grows native and in abundance. Pacific willow (*Salix lucida lasiandra*) is the American west coast's equivalent of alder buckthorn, and charcoal from pacific willow has been a favorite of amateur fireworks hobbyists for many years. It is reported to be, in a number of documented tests, the "fastest" charcoal for gunpowder. I have found it to give excellent results as a propellant powder, leaving minimal fouling and having great strength. As pacific willow is abundant along the edges of rivers and streams around my home, it is also a very convenient wood to use. Like alder buckthorn, it grows as a shrub into a small tree, though rather more quickly.

There is some debate over seasoning of wood to be turned into charcoal for gunpowder. Historically the wood was stacked in piles and seasoned for two or three years, although in 1870 they decided "there appears to be no reason whatever" for requiring several years aging. The only absolute requirement was that "all the moisture in the wood should be expelled before it is placed in the cylinders to be converted into charcoal." Being stacked for a few months in the summer was deemed to be sufficient, and the wood was found to stop decreasing in weight after only two or three months in the mild English summer. I have had considerable success making charcoal from the deadfall of pacific willow, and I have also made charcoal from wood branches that I cut fresh from the tree after aging only about three weeks. The intense heat of the Southern California summer probably drove the moisture out of the wood more completely than an entire English summer. I think three reasonably warm months is adequate aging for any wood fresh cut from the tree; deadfall could probably be picked up and turned into charcoal the same day.

The wood must be clean and "perfectly free from bark." Great importance was placed on removing all traces of bark from the wood used at Waltham Abbey. Decades of experience had determined that bark is a disadvantageous impurity, and a serious cause of fouling residue. I rip the bark away and use a sharp knife if necessary to cut away any bits that cling to the wood, leaving only the clear, clean wood remaining.

The size of the wood must be consistent. English charcoal was made from sticks of alder buckthorn wood one inch in diameter, in "long slender rods." If woods of different sizes are converted to charcoal together, the smaller pieces may be overcooked (for lack of a better term), and the larger pieces may not be cooked enough. Ensuring that the wood is all generally the same size helps considerably with consistency of the charcoal.

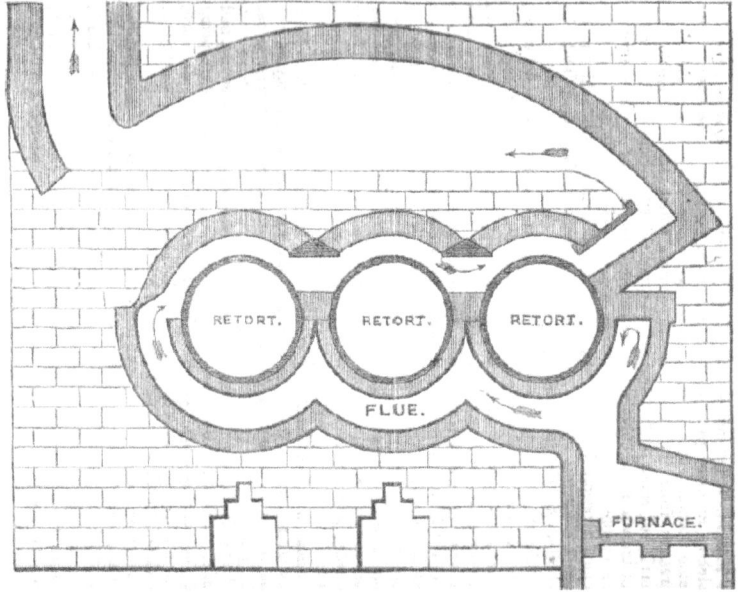

Section of the retort furnace used at Waltham Abbey. The iron "slips" fit into the circular areas labeled *retort*. Heat circulated entirely around the slips.

There were (and are) many popular ways to make charcoal but by the mid-19th century the practice of making it in cylindrical retorts in a large dedicated furnace had become the universal method across the whole of Europe. The wood was loaded into a cylindrical iron container, which was then slid into the retort and tight-fitting iron doors were closed to seal the chamber. Heat from the furnace passed through a flue to pass completely around the retort, ensuring that the heat surrounded the iron cylinder containing the wood and did not just heat it up from one side only. The iron cylinders were known as *slips* at Waltham Abbey, and were three feet long. Bundles of wood were cut to just under three feet, and the slips were filled completely with wood. An iron carriage was used to move the slips to the retorts, at just the right height to be pushed inside, and the heavy iron doors secured shut.

When heated, the wood inside the slip began to give off gas and tar; this was conducted through a pipe and back around into the flue, where it ignited, and was "found greatly to economize fuel," the charcoal contributing to its own production. The flame from the pipe conducting the wood gas was observed, and after 2 or 3 hours or a little more, the flame changed in color to "a violet tint, indicating the formation of carbonic oxide." Once the violet-colored flame was observed, the doors were opened and the slips quickly removed and lowered into sealed iron chambers called "extinguishers," sealed off against any air getting in. The charcoal remained in the extinguishers for a day, before being taken out, the slips emptied, and the charcoal sent into store, ready for the next step of the manufacturing process.

While Waltham Abbey had the benefit of large purpose-built retorts, I do not. My first charcoal making, with the pepper tree wood, was in a cookie tin with the lid wired shut with bailing wire, and a small hole punched through the lid. The cookie tin went into a fire pit, and within a few moments a jet of wood gas pulsed out of the hole. I waited until it stopped producing gas, and pulled the tin out of the fire. Without a doubt, I had exposed the wood to far too high a temperature, and kept it exposed to heat for far too long; this charcoal made abysmal gunpowder. Overheating the charcoal, and keeping it exposed to heat for too long, is just as bad if not worse than underheating.

There are many good plans for making a charcoal retort available online, and several videos on YouTube, although I have never made one to any of these designs. I probably should have, and I admit that the system I am about to describe is probably not very efficient, and produces only a modest quantity of charcoal. But it is good charcoal, and in small batches I have learned, by observation and smell and even sound, a reasonably consistent method.

For several years, I have been using one gallon paint cans as my *slips* and a backyard barbecue grill as my retort. The amount of wood that can fit into the paint cans is not very much, but I find it to be enough for about a pound and a half (perhaps two pounds) of gunpowder. I buy the paint cans new and clean. At first I bought them retail at a local painter's supply store, and the paint cans came with wire handles, as they typically do. I have since discovered paint cans without handles (on an obscure online shopping website called Amazon) and they fit better in my improvised retort. I fill the cans as completely full as I can with wood. I try to select pacific willow branches about one inch thick, but never any larger. If I end up with some branches that are smaller than an inch, I will gather them up and fill a can with them. The important thing is to ensure all the wood in the can is of approximately the same age since cutting and the same diameter; depending on the size of the wood, it will require more or less "cooking" time in the retort. The lids of the paint cans are securely tapped into place; if they are too loose they are liable to pop off, and if this happens over the heat, once oxygen gets inside the charcoal will all ignite and the entire batch is lost.

I have found that a very cheap cylindrical barbeque grill conveniently holds two paint cans lined up in a row forming one long cylinder, which rest on a bailing wire grating that took all of ten minutes to form. Essentially the same model of cheap Chinese-made cylindrical barbeque that I use is available on Amazon for $60, but can probably be found at a garage sale or an old forgotten one stacked in the garage somewhere. I put a small hole (about a quarter inch) in the center of the lids of the paint cans, to allow the gases to vent out. So far, I haven't found a way to direct the wood gases back down below the cans, to add to the heat. I tried once to solder a bit of flexible copper refrigerator tubing to the lid, but the heat simply melted the cheap soft solder the first time I put it in the barbeque retort (duh!), and the tubing promptly fell off. I am sure there is a way to do it, with a mechanical fitting or other method, but it is certainly not necessary.

The fuel I use for heating my retort is actually also pacific willow. There is so much of it, especially very dry piles of deadfall, that I gather up enough for turning into charcoal *and* for supplying the heat for the process. I have also added charcoal briquettes to try to get a steadier and more even heat; they work well but also cost money, and sometimes have struggled to get the required amount of heat. The fire under the paint can "slips" should be kept as low as possible, and trying to hasten the process by increasing heat will only result in overburnt charcoal that makes very poor gunpowder. Low, steady, fairly long term heat is ideal. A magnetic flue thermometer is useful. The temperature inside the paint cans should not get too high, certainly never over 1000° Fahrenheit. Supposedly, 610° Fahrenheit is the "perfect" heat for making charcoal with alder buckthorn. A range from 650° to 800° is generally agreed by the period sources to be good for producing quality propellant charcoal. I have considered adding thermal insulation in the form of fireproof flue or chimney insulation around the barbeque, to retain more heat and act more like an oven (or a true retort) rather than a grill. This, I believe, would make it easier to hold the required temperature, use less fuel, take less time, and produce more consistent charcoal.

As the wood heats up in the paint cans, gases and tars

are driven off and once it really gets going, it shoots out of the hole in the lids of the paint cans like a jet. Sometimes it will ignite, although if I keep the fire fairly low, it will ignite intermittently. Some people think igniting the gas helps with the carbonization. At any rate, inside the retort (barbeque), it sounds like a hellish rocket and can actually get quite loud at the moment of the maximum production of wood gas. In the large retorts at the historic powder mills, the slips were not rotated during the carbonization process, and it was not really necessary because the heat circulated fully around them. In my barbecue retort, I will sometimes turn the paint cans at about an estimated two-thirds of the way through, to ensure that any wood that was at the top is allowed to fully carbonize. The barbeque does not circulate the heat as well as the purpose built retort at Waltham Abbey.

There is a significant question of time and temperature in the charcoal making process. I have a crude simple thermometer that came installed in my cheap barbeque, but I do not rely on it and it does not go high enough. Perhaps as a rough guide it can help, and if the temperature gets far too high, it can let you know when to back it off. A magnetic flue thermometer is a much better option, but again, I would not rely solely on the reading of the thermometer to determine the doneness or quality of the charcoal. I tried to keep the temperature around 750° Fahrenheit inside the barbeque-retort, but if I followed the thermometer only instead of closely watching the volume and force of gas coming out of the paint cans, it inevitably resulted in poor batches. Making charcoal for gunpowder is an art. Thermometers were used at most European charcoal retorts, but not at Waltham Abbey, where "the process is entrusted to the experience and careful watching of the foreman." In the broad scheme of things, I have not made that much charcoal for gunpowder, and probably only a few dozen times, but that is enough to get a basic understanding of what works and what doesn't work, and the signs, smells, and sounds to expect when done right. Knowing what to see, smell, and hear is most important, but a thermometer can add some useful additional information.

I take the charcoal off the heat when the jet of wood gas coming out of the vent hole has subsided considerably from its maximum. Turning the cans may prompt a brief resurgence of gas, but only for a minute or so. The right moment to take the charcoal off the heat is very delicate. Too soon, and the charcoal may not be completely done, and too late, and it is at risk of being overdone. There is no timer or gauge or meter that can determine when the charcoal is perfectly done, that only comes of experience and "getting the knack of it." I've tried to look for the telltale violet color of flame, but since I make my charcoal outdoors with the retort usually in direct sunlight, it is difficult to discern slight variations in colors. The violet color comes from carbon monoxide (carbonic oxide in 19th century chemical terms), and when cooked charcoal begins to give off mostly carbon monoxide, it is an indication that it is done for propellant purposes. Most commercial charcoal makers, who don't use the charcoal as a component of powder, will keep it on the heat until all the oils and tars are driven from the wood. We want the charcoal to be at a perfect point in between being underdone with visible reddish wood fiber remaining, but not overdone with too much of the wood fiber completely carbonized.

My unsolicited, unscientific, personal theory: superior black powder is made from charcoal that still contains some tars and oils that have not been completely removed. This is especially true in terms of fouling. A "fully cooked" charcoal, that has been prepared at high temperature and has a very high percentage of carbon content, will not have any of the creosote or tars remaining (or very little), and while it will probably still work in gunpowder and give satisfactory velocities, it will be a "dry burning" powder. By using fairly low heat and stopping the carbonization a little earlier, the charcoal retains some of the creosote, oils, and tar that will leave softer, wet-looking fouling in the gun. This fouling is not hard, and loading subsequent rounds will be easy and smooth. It is the mark of a truly excellent powder, perfectly suited for the military muzzleloading rifle-musket and the first generations of breechloading black powder cartridge rifles.

Every conceivable method and variation of processes for making charcoal for gunpowder has been tried. Experimentation was done by all the Powers of Europe, and in the United States, for much of the 19th century. Numerous patents for devices and schemes for making better charcoal were issued by several governments. Plans for heating charcoal consistently with superheated steam were actually put into use in France. Charcoal made this way, at a fairly low temperature, had a reddish-brown color and produced higher velocities. "Charcoal prepared between 500° and 600° Fahrenheit has a brown color (*charbon roux*) and although it is more easily inflamed than the black powder charcoal obtained at higher temperatures, its employment in gunpowder is not advantageous. The *charbon roux* is very hygroscopic." Studies were made on the best temperatures for carbonization, and what effect changes in temperatures over the course of carbonization would have. There is some late 19th century research that suggests better gunpowder is made from charcoal that is prepared at a moderate constant temperature for the first three hours, and then at increased temperature for the final twenty minutes or so. In spite of all the research and experiments, the proposed improvements and changes did not produce a gunpowder that was remarkably better than the original mass-produced version, and the method of making charcoal in the conventional retorts, in iron slips, remained nearly universal until the end of black powder's use as a military propellant.

The vent hole in the lid should be covered right away after the container of finished charcoal is removed from the heat. If the hole is not covered up, air will be sucked inside by the charcoal. Hot charcoal desperately wants to ignite and combust, but is prevented by the absence of oxygen. If any air is allowed to get in, the charcoal will light instantly. I set the cans on the ground and cover the hole with a small piece of wood or leather, and place a lead weight on top. Historically, clay was often used to cover up the vents on the slips to prevent the air getting in. Once removed from the heat, the charcoal makes a curious sound as it cools in the absence of air; little clicks and delicate tinkling noises that will eventually stop as it cools. I only make two paint cans of charcoal at a time, which represents very small batches, and is admittedly not efficient in time or fuel. The barbeque retort is still hot, and if I had prepared more paint cans of wood, they could go right in after the others were taken out. My objective is quality, however, and if I was going to attempt anything like large scale production, paint cans and backyard barbeques would never suffice. With a larger retort, one that could hold a hundred pounds of wood or more, enough charcoal for two hundred pounds of powder could be made in an afternoon.

After at least several hours (overnight is even safer) I can pry the paint cans open and remove the finished, cool charcoal. Charcoal can surprise you, and a can of charcoal cooling for well over an hour suddenly started making noises again when the lid was opened and oxygen got in. The yield, depending on the species of wood used and the duration and temperature of charring, is about 25% of the weight of the wood that went into the can. Potassium nitrate is known to be hygroscopic, and will draw moisture from the atmosphere, but contrary to some fervently held popular beliefs, the chief culprit behind black powder's notorious thirst is the charcoal. It aggressively, insatiably wants to draw moisture back into its dry, porous cellular structures. I pour my charcoal directly out of the paint can into a heavy plastic freezer bag, squeeze as much of the air out as I can, and seal it up.

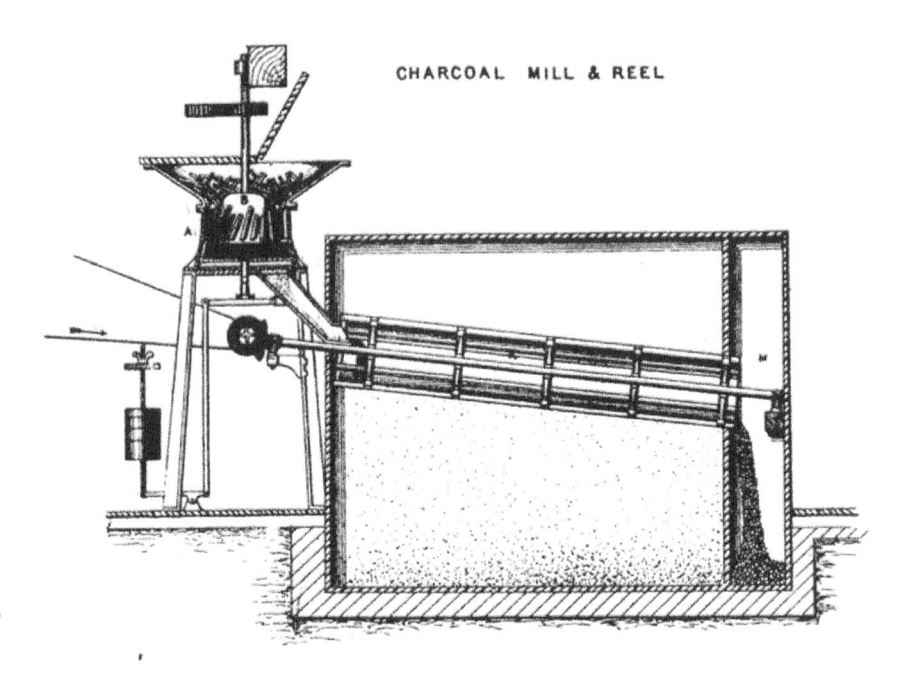

Mill for grinding up charcoal sticks and sifting out fine particles ready for the next step of the process, as used at Waltham Abbey. The grinding mill resembled an oversize coffee mill.

Good charcoal for gunpowder will have certain qualities and physical characteristics. Waltham Abbey considered well-made charcoal to be "jet-black in color, its fracture should show a clear, velvet-like surface, and it should be light and sonorous when dropped on a hard surface." If heated for too long or at too high temperature, the charcoal will become hard and dense, and consist of a much higher percentage of carbon. On the other hand, if not heated long enough or at sufficient temperature, the charcoal "is at once known by its reddish brown color." A very slight tinge of red is acceptable and perhaps even desirable, but this tinge is only visible at certain angles and by no means should jump out as a distinctive feature. It is very hard to explain through text, and like so many other parts of the art of gunpowder making, can really only be known from experience.

Next, the charcoal needs to be broken up and ground down into small pieces. Historically this was done by a charcoal grinding mill at all the government and commercial gunpowder manufactories of the 19th century. It was (and certainly remains) an extremely messy and somewhat unpleasant task, due to the unavoidable mess of the charcoal dust. I bust up charcoal perhaps a couple times a year; the workers in the many enormous gunpowder mills of Europe and the Americas did this every day. One contemporary account describes a visit to a gunpowder mill. "The charcoal mill," the writer said, lies within a "cloud of black dust that flies and floats around in all directions. The faces of the men, as well as their dresses, are of a peculiar, dull, dry black, amid which their eyes shine with a strange intelligence." At mills like Waltham Abbey, the sticks of charcoal were taken out of the iron slips from the retort and laboriously "hand picked to guard against the introduction of any fragments of foreign matter and underburnt knots of wood." While this may seem like an unnecessary step, the considerable cost in time and labor was actually a matter of life and death significance. Anything in the charcoal, such as a piece of iron, a bit of rock, a scrap of wire, etc., could cause a spark later on in the process, and result in catastrophic explosion with great loss of life.

Once carefully sifted through by hand, the charcoal sticks were fed into a machine that used a grinding mechanism similar to old-fashioned coffee mills to crush the charcoal into smaller bits. The broken-up fragments then slid down a rotating reel covered in fine wire mesh (32-mesh), through which the small pieces of charcoal would pass. Any pieces that were too large to go through the mesh were gathered up and run through the mill again, and the process repeated as many times as necessary until it was all small enough to fall through the mesh. As already mentioned, this was ridiculously messy. Powdered charcoal went everywhere. It truly must have been an appalling work experience. Men and boys worked these mills for many hours a day, six days every week, although there is some consolation in the fact that pay for gunpowder mill workers was quite good, and in some cases nearly double the average pay for a laborer.

For my charcoal, I crush it carefully while still in the heavy plastic freezer bags that I store it in. Occasionally this will poke a little hole through the plastic and emit a jet of dust, so I always do this outside or in a nearly abandoned gardening shed. No matter how careful I am, some will get out. As I write this, I honestly can't quite remember what I use to crush the bags with, which means I must have grabbed whatever was handy and tapped lightly, but with just enough force to break up the charcoal pieces and reduce them into smaller pieces. Once broken down, I let the bag sit for a minute or two so that some of the dust can settle before pouring it out (this probably doesn't really help all that much).

At this point I should introduce some of my most useful tools, which were worth the investment. I shelled out the money for a set of stacking sieve buckets with mesh bottoms, each of the four buckets having a different size mesh. They could be made from scratch easily enough with some wood and mesh, but at the time, it was a lot more practical for me to click "Buy Now" than actually make them. Cheap versions can be found for under $30 that will probably do good enough; I splurged a bit and got the nicer quality set that was designed to fit neatly over a 5-gallon plastic bucket, and I have not regretted this. In fact, it would be ideal to have several sets of these sieve buckets, for use with different components and mixtures. My method of making powder involves a lot of sifting out of powders. I pour my charcoal into the sieve bucket with the finest mesh (also approximately a 32-mesh). Only the very finest charcoal that passes through the finest mesh sieve is saved for the next step; everything else will go back into the ziplock bag for more crushing, and will get sieved again, saving the fine pieces that pass through. Eventually, I am left with a measure of charcoal dust, and fortunately only a few ounces are required to make several pounds of powder.

Crushing and sifting charcoal is absurdly messy. I wear goggles and a respirator and do this inside the semi-abandoned garden shed because any hint of wind or moving air will grab the charcoal dust and fling it about wildly, robbing me of all my effort in making the charcoal so far. The charcoal dust coats everything within reach in a fine film, including (if I let it) my hair, eyes, teeth, and probably my soul.

5
SULFUR

Of the three components of gunpowder, sulfur is (mercifully) the most simple and most easily acquired in a pure and usable state. Today, it is available in cheap abundance because it is a byproduct of gasoline refining, and the distillation of gasoline also results in surprisingly pure sulfur. It can be found on the internet, in pure powdered form, for a couple dollars a pound, although I am careful to make sure it's ordinary elemental sulfur, and not sublimed (also called flowers of sulfur). My grandmother used to sprinkle that stuff on her roses.

Sulfur is also what gives gunpowder its characteristic rotten egg smell. Brimstone serves several functions in the composition. Captain Smith tells us "the value of sulfur as an ingredient of gunpowder is due to the low temperature at which it inflames." By lowering the ignition temperature of gunpowder, sparks from flintlocks will set it off; primers and percussion caps can also use a modest quantity of percussive material. It is generally accepted that sulfur's unique bonding characteristics help hold the triumvirate of ingredients together, although the once-popular theory that sulfur bonds with the nitrate to "fill the pores" of the charcoal has largely been disproven. Another important role of sulfur is in raising the heat of the gases generated when gunpowder burns. Gases take up greater volume when at higher temperatures, and this directly equates to stronger gunpowder and higher velocities.

Sulfur was not easy to get in the 19th century. Nearly everybody (even the United States, for long periods) imported sulfur from the volcanic earth of southern Italy and Sicily. Waltham Abbey imported the highest quality sulfur known as *Licara firsts*, which was about 95% pure. It was purified again at Waltham Abbey by distillation, which rendered it virtually 100% pure. Then it was reduced to a somewhat coarse powder and also sifted through 32-mesh sieves. Have a moment to consider the men employed at this task. A visitor to an English powder mill recalled that "the most striking feature of this house is the ghastly faces of the men, whose eyes seem to look out of a grim, yellowish mask."

I do not purify the sulfur, and buy it at an asserted 99.5% purity. Two pounds of sulfur is enough for 20 pounds of gunpowder. It comes already ground into a powder and needs no further attention from me before being measured out for mixing and incorporation.

Sulfur is the least essential component of gunpowder and while it has some advantageous effects, it also contributes to a great deal of fouling residue and corrosive acids. Making a successful gunpowder without sulfur was the goal of many scientists for two centuries, but in all cases, gunpowder with sulfur provided demonstrably better results than gunpowder made without it. French revolutionary scientists tried very hard to make a saltpeter-charcoal mixture work, when their supply of Italian sulfur was interrupted by the wars. They were not successful, and brimstone must still be part of the mischievous discovery.

6
INCORPORATION

We come at last to the point where separate components, painstakingly prepared with much time and labor, finally come together. The process of mixing the nitrate, charcoal, and sulfur and incorporating them together is the most crucial, and the most attendant with danger. It marks the transition point from three inert ingredients being converted into a highly energetic substance. For that reason, this will be the longest chapter. There is a lot to explain, and I also feel there is an important historic context that illuminates the various methods in use today by amateur enthusiasts who make powder for propellant purposes.

Engineering magazine in 1878 explained that "the incorporation, or grinding together, of the three ingredients that form gunpowder is by far the most important process in the whole manufacture." Captain Smith was even more elaborate:

> Incorporation is unquestionably the most important of all the operations in the manufacture of

gunpowder. Saltpeter, sulfur, and charcoal goes into the incorporating mill a mere mixture and leaves it gunpowder. Nothing that can be done to it afterwards will add to its strength of explosiveness; no future treatment can remedy defective incorporation. By incorporation is, of course, meant the long-continued grinding together of the ingredients, which blends them together and brings them into such close juxtaposition that they appear to form a new substance. Unless this be done perfectly, perfect mutual decomposition of the constituents of the gunpowder cannot be expected, on combustion. The more thoroughly it is effected the stronger will be the resulting gunpowder.

Mixing and incorporation were two separate, distinct steps at Waltham Abbey. As discussed in a previous chapter, the proportions used at Waltham Abbey were by weight 75 parts of saltpeter, 15 parts charcoal, and 10 of sulfur. The components were carefully weighed out to make a combined total of 50 pounds (that is to say, 37.5 pounds of saltpeter, 7.5 pounds of charcoal, and 5 pounds of sulfur). The saltpeter was used "wet" at Waltham Abbey, containing several percent of moisture, and this was taken into account to ensure the correct proportion of potassium nitrate would be in the finished product, and not a few percent short once the moisture was removed. This went into a mixing machine, which consisted of "a hollow drum of copper about 2 feet wide by 3 feet in diameter, which is made to revolve at a speed of thirty-five revolutions per minute." Inside this copper drum were several rows of contra rotating arms, which spun around an axle running through the drum. While the drum itself rotated, the arms inside also spun at a rate of 70 RPM. It worked, essentially, like a somewhat more complicated kitchen mixer; the only purpose was to thoroughly mix all three ingredients together. The machine did this in about five minutes.

Once mixed, the powder was taken out of the drum and passed through an 8-mesh sieve, being carefully screened by hand, checking once more for any foreign objects. The screened powder was put into 50 pound bags and tied up very tightly, because each component of the mixture had different specific gravities, and if kept loose, the saltpeter would settle to the bottom and the charcoal rise to the top, and defeat the entire purpose of the mixing machine.

This mixed composition was called a green charge because the granules of sulfur in it gave the grayish mixture a somewhat greenish-yellow tinge. This was also the first point in the manufacturing process that the material was hazardous. The freshly mixed ingredients were not yet truly gunpowder, but even in this state the green charge could be ignited, and it would flash in a messy and inefficient explosion. In 1867, there was a fire in the mixing house of an English commercial powder mill that killed four workmen. "The bodies of the victims," Captain Smith wrote, "are generally found to be more burnt than those of men killed by explosions of gunpowder."

Now it was ready for the incorporation mill. In every 19th century British source, incorporation is universally named as the most essential to the production of quality powder. "Upon the thorough and effectual incorporation which it receives depends mainly the excellence of English powder," Captain Smith observes. "Great attention is paid to the process in this country, not only for military but for sporting purposes, and the most powerful mills are always used. It has been carried to the highest pitch of excellence." It is indisputable that Captain Smith was correct, and here I repeat again my conviction that English gunpowder in the second half of the 19th century was probably the best ever made at a large scale.

The green meal was incorporated by an edge-runner mill, which consisted of a pair of enormously heavy mill wheels attached to a central axis that they rotated about over a strong circular bed with raised edges, forming something of a bowl. The wheels were sometimes made out of stone, especially in older mills, but by the 1860s they were usually iron. The earliest iron mill-wheels (called runners) were given a bronze tire to avoid any sparks; later, regular iron runners were used. Regardless of the material they were made out of, the runners were incredibly heavy. At some powder mills in India, the runners weighed six tons each. Waltham Abbey used runners of 3.5 or 4 tons each and were seven feet in diameter.

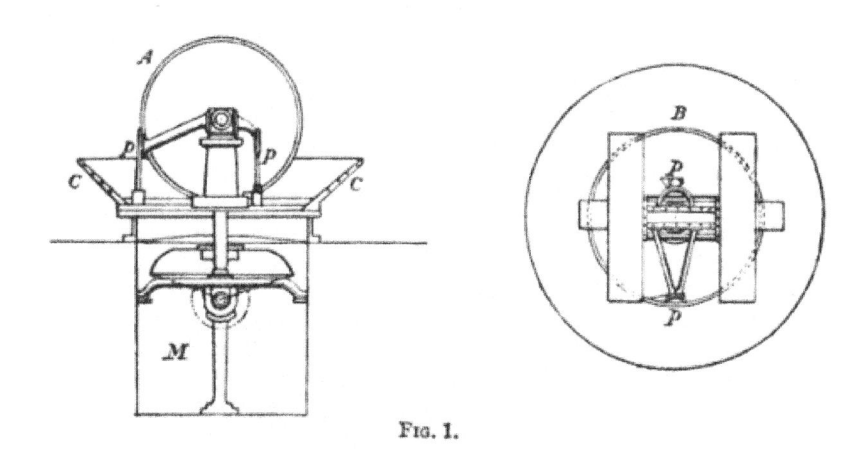

Fig. 1.

Section and elevation of an edge runner mill, similar to those used at Waltham Abbey and other powder mills, both then and now.

The function of these mills was to simultaneously grind down the green charge of powder into infinitesimally small particles, and physically squash these particles together until the powder was transformed from a mixture of three separate components into a homogenous new substance: gunpowder. Driving extremely heavy millstones or iron runners over the composition accomplished this extremely well. Edge-runner mills are still used to this day in the production of black powder, and before the factory was closed in 2021, edge-runner incorporation mills were used at the GOEX plant in Minden, Louisiana. If the plant ever re-opens, the edge-runner mills will almost certainly be used again.

Engraving of an edge-runner mill, showing the raised edges of the iron bed, and the machinery used to rotate the runners.

An Act of Parliament restricted the amount of powder that could be incorporated by a single edge-runner mill at a time to 50 pounds. This did something to reduce the catastrophic effect of a powder explosion in the incorporating mill, and perhaps limit its propagation to nearby mills. At Waltham Abbey, a 50-pound sack of green charge was poured onto the bed and evened out with wooden rakes, the workmen making absolutely certain that there was plenty of powder lying in front of the runners. The mill was advanced a quarter turn, and any empty space now behind the runners was filled back in. Once the green charge was evenly distributed, it was moistened with a small amount of water. The amount of water used was left to the judgment of the senior workman at the mill, whose many years of experience and knowledge led him to put exactly the right amount of water onto the powder. In damp weather only two or three pints were sprinkled on from a brass watering-can with a very fine head, but in hotter and drier weather, eight to ten pints were sometimes added. This process was known as liquoring.

Before the mill was started, the workmen left the building. Nobody remained inside the millhouses while they were in operation, due to the risk of explosion. A massive amount of friction was present, with many tons of iron or stone pressing down on a bed of powder that was only about two inches thick. If the iron runners were ever to touch the iron bed, there would almost certainly be a spark and cause an explosion. The only thing preventing an explosion was the actual powder in the mill itself, a curious and somewhat ironic instance of a highly inflammable and explosive material preventing its own ignition by the mass of its own substance serving as a barrier between the iron. As the runners turned, a plow covered in leather traveled immediately in front of them and would shove the powder back into the direct path of the runner. The runners completed eight revolutions per minute

Explosions during the milling were relatively common, so much so that the buildings containing the incorporating mills had three strong walls and the fourth very lightly made of a thin sheet metal or wood, with a lightweight and simple roof. If the powder blew, the millhouse would remain intact and the roof and wall quickly replaced. Each mill also had an automatic fire extinguishing device, holding many gallons of water, suspended directly above them. If there was an explosion in one of the mills, the "drenching apparatus" would detect the blast by a mechanical shutter, and dump the water. This system worked so well that operations could be resumed as soon as two hours after an explosion.

Small arms powder was milled for 4 hours; cannon powder was only milled for 3. After this time, with occasional liquorings, the powder had ceased to be a true powder at all and was now in the form of what was called *mill cake*, a mostly-solid half-inch thick cake of gunpowder. At eight revolutions per minute, the mill cake would have been passed over 3,840 times by the heavy runners. Because the runners were turning in a circle around an axis, they imparted a slight rotary grinding onto the mass while pressing down with much force. After four hours, the mill cake was done: "the cake should be of a blackish gray color, and when broken, of a uniform appearance, without any white or yellow specks in it, the presence of these would indicate insufficient incorporation or grinding." It was now true gunpowder. "At the expiration of three or four hours," *Engineering* magazine described in 1878, "the charge will have attained all the properties of gunpowder."

Testing the mixture was done by igniting a very small quantity on a glass plate. All that should be left is a black sooty mark. Any presence of small white or yellow beads or specks indicates that it has not been fully incorporated.

When milling was done, workers used wooden tools to scrape the mill cake up from the bed and put it into wooden tubs, to be taken away for breaking-up and pressing. This was hazardous work and could not be done remotely. A spark was instantly fatal. To guard against sparks, the workers wore india-rubber overshoes and suits of "incombustible clothing, leather caps and gloves." The floors of the incorporating millhouses were covered in leather or animal hides, and kept damp. Everything was covered in gunpowder dust. Fortunately, the precautions were effective and accidents while workers were inside the millhouse were relatively rare.

That was the Waltham Abbey method of incorporation, and also that of the major powder makers of the latter 19th century. It has proven to be so superior in quality of final product and economy of production that it remains in use today.

The hobbyist, however, has a problem. I don't have a massive edge-runner incorporation mill with six-ton grinding stones. If the incorporation of the powder is *the* essential, crucial step of the entire process, can any powder be made by the simple-tooled hobbyist that even remotely approaches the quality and performance of the historic gunpowder? The answer is yes... sort of.

Grinding, mixing, and incorporating powder under a massive weight of many tons for many hours is not a possibility for me and almost certainly never will be. There is another way, and although the alternatives are by no means to be considered the equal of the edge-runner incorporation mill, they can produce a powder that is very nearly the equivalent of the excellent 19th century propellant powders.

Today, this alternative method is almost universally known as *ball milling*. At its most basic form, it uses a dense media (usually hardened lead, but sometimes ceramic or other materials) to grind a material down into smaller and smaller sizes by spinning it together in a drum. As the drum spins, the grinding media and the composition being milled will collide, and abrasion and friction between the media will steadily reduce the particle size of the composition. Extremely fine powders can be produced in ball mills.

The ball mill method of mixing and incorporating gunpowder was introduced during the French Revolution in the early 1790s. As the French found themselves at war with nearly all of Europe, enormous quantities of gunpowder were required, and the existing French powder mills could not produce a fraction of the demand. The famous French chemist Lavoisier, who high school students know as "the father of modern chemistry," made dramatic improvements to French powder production before he went to the guillotine in 1794 for the unspeakable and probably invented crime of adding water to tobacco. In France, gunpowder was incorporated and formed into something like millcake by *stamp mills*. A somewhat inferior powder was formed by the *fabriquée par le procédé des pilons*. These were essentially mechanized mortars and pestles, and rows of them would pound at the mixture of powder in a mortar, for as long as 24 hours. Batches were quite small, and involved considerable manual labor to add and remove the powder from the mortars. This powder was not pressed, and it was instead broken up into grains after the beaten cake was removed from the stamp mills. It transported very poorly and fell apart into dust. Although the French clung to the stamp mill process all the way until the Franco-Prussian War of 1870, a French journal in 1879 dolefully acknowledged that stamp mill powder was really only suitable for smoothbore guns.

Jacques-Pierre Champy succeeded Lavoisier in 1794, and one of his pupils was Du Pont, who would build a gunpowder mill in the United States in 1801. (Du Pont gunpowder was produced in the United States until the 1970s, when the factory was purchased by GOEX, and later moved to Louisiana, where production continued until 2021.) Another associate of Champy was Jean-Antoine Carny, who introduced a new method of gunpowder production at the major French powder mill at Grenelle. For its association with the French Revolution, over the next hundred years Carny's method would be known as the "revolutionary process" of milling gunpowder.

The revolutionary method is described well by an English source in 1816:

> The French not only improved the process of purifying nitre, but also the manufacture of gunpowder, so much that the powder works of Grenelle alone fabricated 34,000 lbs of gunpowder daily... To produce a still more perfect grinding and mixture, the powder is now put into strong casks of oak-plank, which have ledges or mouldings on their inside, similar to those of a barrel churn. These casks are mounted upon iron axles, which are covered with wood; about 75lbs of the composition is put in at a time, and 80lbs of bronze small balls about 4 lignes [3/8 inches, or 9mm] in diameter. The cask being now put into a very rapid motion by means of machinery, the collision of the balls and the violent agitation of the composition soon effects its complete trituration and mixture. The composition is known to be sufficiently pulverized when a little of it being spread on a pallet with a smooth knife, no signs of roughness appear.

After being milled in the casks for a modest length of time, perhaps three or four hours, the mixture was taken out, wetted slightly, and pressed on a screw-press. This was a very well mixed and reasonably well incorporated powder, and when pressed it formed hard, durable grains. It was not only superior in power and performance than stamp mill powder, but much faster and cheaper to make. In fact, it worked so well that it was adopted across all of France even after the explosion of the gunpowder factory at Grenelle on 31 August 1794, which killed over 500 people and remains one of the worst industrial accidents in French history.

Carny's revolutionary ball mill method reduced the powder to an extremely fine dust and mixed it thoroughly well. It could not fully incorporate the gunpowder in the same powerful way as the English incorporating mill, however. Keep in mind that the ingredients for English powder went into the mixing machine, and then to the incorporating mill, with the sulfur and charcoal fairly coarse, having been sifted through a 32-mesh screen. The heavy runners of the mill would crush the pieces of sulfur and charcoal down into a very fine consistency, and then as the runners went round and round, all three ingredients were forced into an intimate unity under the pressure of the weight and the slight twisting motion of the wheels. Carny's ball mill accomplished only half of the work done by the English incorporating mills. The revolutionary method reduced all three ingredients to a very fine dust, as fine as talcum powder, but it did not force the ingredients together with the same weight, power, and grinding motion of the English mills.

Even so, the revolutionary method produced a perfectly serviceable powder and soon Napoleon's armies had conquered nearly all of Europe with it. After the Peace, stamp mills briefly made an abortive return to France, and many French authorities insisted that gunpowder produced by stamp mills caused less erosion or abrasion on guns. Some Frenchmen refused to believe that English powder could be so good, and in the 1830s a French artillery captain insisted that English powder makers were "charlatans" who were secretly adding fulminate of mercury to make it stronger. Eventually the obvious superiority of the edge-runner incorporation mill won out, and in the 1870s they were finally in common use in France.

This was not the end of the ball mill, however. The French, the Prussians, and even the British gunpowder mills in India continued to use Carny's revolutionary ball mill method to intimately mix the ingredients and reduce them to an extremely fine consistency. The Indian powder mills used workmen to turn the barrels of powder and bronze balls, manual labor being cheaper in India than steam or water power. In most countries, the ball mill was used to mix and grind the power, and then this well-mixed and extremely fine mixture went over to the incorporating mill, to be ground and pressed under the runners just like at Waltham Abbey. It was a combination of the two methods, and did indeed produce an excellent powder. Even the United States, after the American Civil War, adopted exactly this system of ball milling the ingredients into a very fine powder before the incorporation mill.

The method I use to mix and incorporate my powder cannot accurately be called the Waltham Abbey method, because I don't have the incorporation mill. Here, my methods irrevocably must deviate with significance from the historical English process that I have attempted to faithfully follow. The lack of a massive incorporating mill makes this unavoidable.

One other European country continued to use Carny's revolutionary method well into the middle 19th century: Prussia. The popular "ball mill then press" method of making black powder, which is discussed and described all over the internet and in countless books on amateur pyrotechnics, is actually the *Prussian* method from the mid-1800s. The Prussians did not use incorporating mills with heavy millstones or iron runners. Instead, they mixed and incorporated their powder solely in ball mills before pressing, and the gunpowder manufactured in this way was quite good, by all accounts. It was also proven by the ultimate forge of battle, being used in the Second Schleswig War of 1864, the Austro-Prussian War of 1866, and the Franco-Prussian War of 1870-71. The gunpowder being burned in the barrels of Prussian Dreyse needle-rifles at Königgrätz and Sedan was produced by this method. So, while my method (the Prussian method) deviates from the English production as done at Waltham Abbey, it is still capable of making exceptionally high quality propellant powder that is *almost* the equal of the English powders.

Major Alfred Mordecai visited the Prussian powder mills during the Delafield Commission's tour of Europe, at the time of the Crimean War (1854-1856). In 1860, he submitted his final report and described the Prussian gunpowder production thusly:

> The method of mixing and incorporating the materials is essentially the same as that which is known in France as "the revolutionary process," from its having been adopted as an expeditious method of making gunpowder during the French revolution. In that country it has been discontinued, from a belief that powder made in this way is too destructive to the guns, and not susceptible of good preservation; but probably the modifications introduced in the Prussian method have removed these objections, as it is practised in that country in preference to the stamping mills of France and the [edge roller] mills of England. The method consists of pulverizing the materials in rolling barrels, mixing and incorporating them in the same manner, and forming the cake under a press. These barrels are made of wood and the pulverizing is effected by means of bronze balls five-eights of an inch in diameter; the charge of a barrel being 200 pounds of materials and 200 pounds of balls. The incorporating barrels are made of leather stretched on wooden frames, and the balls used for this purpose are one quarter of an inch to five sixteenths of an inch in diameter.

The Prussians, therefore, both pulverized and incorporated their powder in ball mills. This was a two-step process, with the ingredients being pulverized first in one ball mill, and then combined and incorporated together in another ball mill (made out of leather to further reduce any possibility of a spark). U.S. Ordnance officers visited the gunpowder mill at Spandau in 1873, in what was now Imperial Germany, and found the ball mill method still in full use. The only change was the adoption of "brown charcoal" intended to produce superior performance from the Mauser 1871 rifle.

Another technique was adopted by the French and Prussians in the late 1860s and 1870s: *proportional milling*. When the three ingredients of gunpowder are mixed together in their usual proportions of 75 parts saltpeter, 15 parts charcoal, and 10 parts sulfur, it is an explosive energetic mixture, even in the form of green charge. There is always a significant degree of risk when milling all three powders together in their usual proportions as gunpowder. It was soon realized that *non-explosive* proportions of the ingredients could be mixed and milled together without much fear of explosion or ignition, and thereby reduce them down to an extremely fine powder and incorporate them at the same time. Only as the last step were the materials finally combined to form the 75-15-10 ratio of actual energetic gunpowder, and milled for a much briefer time. It reduced the amount of time an explosive mixture was being milled, and therefore reduced the possibility of an accident. This also served a practical purpose of preventing the individual ingredients from clumping up while being ground in the ball mills.

A description of the "French method" at the Belgian gunpowder mill at Wetteren, written in 1879, is particularly useful. Here, the saltpeter was split up, with one-third of the saltpeter being added to the charcoal and two-thirds being added to the sulfur. Neither mixture is extremely hazardous, as there is not enough nitrate to provide oxygen for the charcoal to burn with explosive rapidity, and the saltpeter/sulfur mix can almost be considered completely inert. These *mélanges binaires*, or binary compositions, were milled together for a fairly long period of time in iron drums with 100 bronze balls. Once reduced to a fairly well incorporated dust, the two binary mixtures were combined to make the *mélange ternaire*, which contained all three components of gunpowder in the energetic proportions. This ternary mixture was milled in another barrel lined with leather, with 50 bronze balls, until well incorporated.

This is essentially what I do for my powder. Ball mills come in all shapes and sizes, for various purposes. There are cheap ones (sometimes marketed as rock tumblers) that will only hold perhaps a couple ounces of material, and very large and expensive ones that can mill many pounds at a time. Many hobbyists make their own ball mills and there are plenty of "How To" websites and videos on the internet. I have had several, starting with the very small ball mill that barely held anything, and some homemade versions. The ball mill that I have used with the most success for milling powder was, in fact, not even intended to be used for powder at all. I bought a mill very similar to a design marketed as "Thumlers Tumbler" to use for wet-polishing spent brass cartridge cases, and ended up never really using it for polishing cases. The heavy-duty steel drum is fully lined with a rubberized insert, with a watertight lid that is held firmly in place with a series of wing nuts. For my purposes, and my very small quantities being milled at a time, it is ideal. The tumbler is marketed to hold 15 pounds, but I never come close to that capacity even with a considerable amount of heavy milling media. The barrel is hexagonal, which provides a great advantage for milling; the material and media are carried up a distance as the barrel rotates, and then is dropped suddenly all at once, grinding the material as it falls and lands. If the barrel was perfectly round, it would have a much more gradual effect, with less efficiency.

There is a lot of discussion and controversy over what milling media to use. While I think there is plenty of room for debate over the best milling media for non-energetic mixtures, I am absolutely convinced that *only* lead media be used when milling any quantity of black powder. I also think anyone who mills black powder with anything other than lead is taking an unacceptable risk. On this point, I don't think there is any room for compromise.

I have used three types of milling media. For milling the ingredients separately or in a non-energetic binary mixture, I have used brass and steel balls. As I just mentioned, for mixing the combined ingredients, I only use hardened antimony lead shot. My lead and steel balls are half inch, and the brass is variously sized but more or less half an inch on average.

Ball mills are notoriously inefficient if overloaded. There must be plenty of room in the grinding barrel for material to *move*. I usually only mill one pound of non-emergetic material at a time, with one or two pounds of media, depending on what I am milling. Too much material and not enough media will lead to inefficient milling and poor results; too much media and not enough material will cause your media to wear down at an excessive rate. Somewhere in between is the ideal middle ground and while there are rules of thumb about material-to-media ratios, nothing is really set in stone.

My process is simple and intended to reduce the inherent hazards to as short a time as possible, and emphasize safety to the greatest possible extent. I will measure out, in separate containers, enough potassium nitrate, charcoal, and sulfur to make one kilogram (a little over two pounds) of gunpowder. Working in metric units makes the calculations a little simpler, since one kilogram can be divided proportionally to 750 grams of potassium nitrate, 150 grams of charcoal, and 100 grams of sulfur. If the potassium nitrate still contains some moisture, I will add a little more (perhaps another 20 grams) to account for the weight of the water that will eventually leave the composition.

Instead of putting all 750 grams of weighed-out potassium nitrate together, I weigh out 200 grams of potassium nitrate into one container (Container #1), and 550 grams into another (Container #2). Then I take the charcoal and weigh out 100 grams that goes into Container #1 with the 200 grams of potassium nitrate, and then the remaining 50 grams of charcoal goes into Container #2. All 100 grams of sulfur goes into Container #1. This results in the first container of 400 grams with a proportion of 2 parts saltpeter to 1 part charcoal and 1 part sulfur, and the second container of 600 grams at a ratio of 11 parts of saltpeter to 1 part charcoal. If ignited, both compositions would burn, but they will not burn *fast* and most importantly, they will not *explode*. There is either not enough charcoal fuel, or not enough potassium nitrate oxidizer, in either mixture to be particularly dangerous. Container #1 is also drowned in sulfur. The advantage of milling the components in this binary arrangement is to achieve a thorough mixing and some degree of preliminary incorporation without a serious risk of an accident.

Weighing out the charcoal is very messy, and must be done inside the semi-abandoned garden shed, lest any slight breeze send a large proportion of it flying away into the air. Even then, some of it will escape. The potassium nitrate needs to be mostly dry, but a slight amount of moisture is acceptable. If it is too wet, the mixture will clump and fail to incorporate.

I am fortunate to have access to a large horse ranch in a sparsely populated unincorporated area, which conveniently has electric power run out to a remote part of the ranch. Out there, in this open space, I have built a "bunker" of three short walls with sandbags. My ball mill sits inside this bunker, and the open end faces the opposite direction that I approach it from. I do all of my milling here, even the binary mixtures, out of a superabundance of caution. The ball mill is started and stopped simply by plugging it in or unplugging it, which enables me to start and stop it remotely from an extension cord. About 45 revolutions per minute is desirable, although a little faster probably wouldn't hurt. The drum should never rotate so quickly that centrifugal force prevents a good milling action, and carries the very light mixture all the way around.

For milling the binary mixtures, I have used brass/bronze and steel media. I still feel safer using the brass, as I do have some concerns about small bits of steel being broken away from the steel media which could end up in the mixture and potentially cause a spark when milling the combined charge. However, the brass wears faster, and is much more expensive than steel media. Obviously, any media material that wears off during the milling process is added to the mixture, and represents an impurity. It is frustrating to have gone to lengths to achieve an absolute purity of ingredients, only to poison the composition with foreign matter from the milling media. From my observations, there is virtually no wear visible on the steel media after very long durations of milling, while wear on the brass/bronze media becomes apparent after a few loads. Steel media should be kept free from any oil, but the potassium nitrate is a powerful oxidizer and if there is moisture in the nitrate, the steel media will want to blossom with rust. Iron oxide is an undesirable contaminant in the powder. If the steel media rusts, I run it in the mill for a while with a couple handfuls of granulated walnut hulls to remove the rust. Using stainless steel media may not rust as fast but the layer of stainless steel will be eventually ground away.

I used to weigh or measure out the milling media in proportion with the material to be milled, but now I simply dump (I actually very slowly pour it, to prevent it raising too much dust) the material into the milling drum, and then (slowly) pour in media a few pieces at a time until it reaches a certain level even with the material. Not so little media that I can't see it through the mixture, and not so much that it covers up the material. This has worked well for me, as unscientific as it is.

Then I secure the lid, and remotely turn on the mill. It makes a rhythmic noise – crunch, crunch, crunch – as the media is dropped again and again by the hexagonal walls of the drum. In time, the grinding of the media will reduce the compositions to the desired end state: an extremely fine powder. I mill my binary mixtures for at least 6 hours. The ranch where I do the milling is a bit of a distance from where I live, but near my church, so I end up doing most of my milling on Sunday afternoons, and doing one binary mixture a day. This means it can take several Sundays to mill enough mixture to make one kilogram (two pounds) of powder. I'm totally fine with this, because I am in no rush and the dragon bites: I keep him small.

When the milling time is done, I remotely turn the mill off and let it sit a while. The mixture inside will be incredibly fine powder. The media is removed by pouring the powder through the largest mesh sieve. Each binary mixture is placed in a carefully labeled plastic container with a lid, and sometimes I even stick the whole container into a freezer bag as an added precaution against the messiest spill in the world, and to make sure I keep out as much air as possible.

Finally comes the time to mix the two binary mixtures together, and this results in a new ternary mixture that is in the proportions of energetic black powder. This is the mischievous discovery, the holy trinity, the dreaded triumvirate of ingredients that forms a composition that shaped our world, raised up civilizations and brought others down. I mill 500 grams at a time. It hardly takes up any space in the ball mill drum, and there is surely room for several more pounds of mixture, but again, I am in no rush.

I use antimony hardened lead media for milling the green charge. Some of this I cast myself, some of it I've bought. The lead should be very well hardened, linotype is a good alloy to use. The harder the lead, the less will be ground away to contaminate the powder. Unfortunately there is no avoiding some small measure of lead contamination. Some people use brass or ceramic media for milling their black powder, and a lot of these people have done this many times with no accidents. Yet, some accidents have been reported. An 8-inch Civil War-era shell was filled with about 500 grams of gunpowder, and I do not want a drum of 500 grams of powder going off, if only because it would ruin my ball mill, which wasn't cheap!

I have varied my milling times with the ternary mixture, and found that longer milling usually results in superior performing propellant powder (higher velocities). This stage of milling is the greatly desired incorporation: the components are mixed, they are ground down to incredibly fine dusts, and now the lead media is pounding the mixture together with hundreds of thousands of small impacts as the ball mill turns the drum. At the same time, longer milling times increase the amount of lead contamination. At some point, the amount of lead contamination in the powder would begin to counteract any benefit of thorough incorporation, but this would probably be after 24 hours (or more), if the lead is very hard. I prefer to mill the powder for at least 4 hours. I have milled it for as short as 2 hours, and this batch of powder gave me velocities about 20% lower than commercial (Swiss) powder. It also showed signs of incomplete incorporation when flashed on glass. After 4 hours, I've found the powder to flash perfectly clean, and it gives me desirable velocities without too much lead contamination.

Removing the milled powder from the drum is probably the most hazardous moment of the whole process. I remotely stop the ball mill and let it settle for a while. I am careful not to handle the drum in a cavalier fashion, with any brisk movements. Normally I carefully tip it open end up and carry it back to my pickup truck, parked a hundred feet or so away from my "milling bunker." Using the bed of the pickup as a shield against any wind, I open the drum and sieve the powder to get the lead balls out. The powder will be extremely fine, and will want to blow everywhere.

This stuff is now gunpowder. It has been mixed and incorporated, and only needs to be pressed, broken up into grains, and dusted. The dragon is fully alive.

7
PRESSING

"The only perfect way of converting gunpowder into serviceable grains without in any degree whatever interfering with the perfect incorporation of the ingredients, is first to compress the soft material into hard masses by pressure alone, and then to crush up these masses into the description of grain required. The object of pressing, then, is to convert the soft dusty mass of incorporated ingredients, now gunpowder, into hard cakes of the particular density which is found to give the best results when the powder is finished." Thus does Captain Smith adequately introduce the purpose and reason of pressing the powder into a hard, dense solid, by means of a powerful press. He also touched on a key word – *density* – which is an aspect of gunpowder that has been almost completely forgotten and neglected by black powder shooters. A U.S. Army artillery textbook in 1893 explained that "the property which exercises the greatest influence upon the general character and action of gunpowder is its *density*," and that "the *density* of the powder, which can be varied at will, must be its *most important physical quality*, or property."

When we last were at Waltham Abbey, the powder had

been ground into a fine dust and thoroughly incorporated under very heavy millstones or iron edge runners. After being subjected to the extreme weight of the runners, the incorporated gunpowder was about half an inch thick and semi-solid. Indeed, gunpowder was considered finished at this point until the introduction of pressed powder at the very end of the 18th century. All the work done by Brown Bess from Ramilles to Yorktown was fueled by a loose and un-pressed gunpowder that was very dusty and totally inconsistent. Only a few decades later, this powder would have been considered woefully unsatisfactory. So after the mill cake was taken out of the bed of the incorporating mill at Waltham Abbey, it went next to a *breaking-down machine* to reduce the mill cake back to a dusty powder, and then it went to the press house to be compressed into a dense solid.

Pressing the powder conveys several benefits, and there are no compelling arguments for *not* pressing gunpowder. The more practical benefits include a stronger grain that will hold up to the rigors of transportation, and even shaking about inside the cartridges carried in the pouches of soldiers on campaign. Pressed powder is much more resistant to absorbing moisture. It can be polished and glazed, knocking away sharp corners so that the powder produces much less dust. Perhaps the paramount advantage is that pressed powder can be made to a single consistency, of known and measurable density, customized to the application for which it is intended.

One famous example of the importance of density is the gunpowder for the Martini-Henry rifle. In the early tests of the new Martini-Henry, the old R.F.G. gunpowder that had worked excellently for the Pattern 1853 Enfield rifle-musket and Snider caused terrible fouling in the new .45-caliber breechloader. After a few shots the Henry rifling clogged with fouling, and the accuracy of the gun fell off. Some critics went so far as to claim this was proof that "small bore" rifles would never work. Captain Smith put it this way: "the tendency of small-bore rifles to foul has long been well known. The Whitworth and Westley-Richards rifles have invariably been found to foul unless fired with special lubricating wads. It seems consequently to have been taken as an ascertained fact that all small bores will foul." Great pains were taken to modify the method and type of lubricant in these early small-bore (usually .45-caliber) rifles, but Captain Smith accurately explained that the problem wasn't with the small-bore rifles themselves, or with the methods of lubricant. "The fault," Captain Smith observed, "which was really one of the powder, had been transferred to the arms. Fouling may be to a great extent, if not entirely, overcome by modifying the density of the powder used. For experience shows that the slower the action of the charge the less likelihood is there of fouling. Slowness of action can of course be obtained at once by increase of density."

The Martini-Henry shot very poorly with R.F.G. powder, but when tried in 1869 using commercially-produced Curtis & Harvey's N o. 6 gunpowder, suddenly most of the fouling issues went away. The No. 6 was a much denser powder than R.F.G., and over the next two years, the Martini-Henry was tested with experimental powders of various densities, hardnesses, and grain size. Finally in May 1872, a specially-developed new powder with a density of 1.745 produced 1328 feet per second of velocity in the Martini-Henry with minimal fouling and a better figure of merit than Curtis & Harvey No. 6. This was declared R.F.G.2 powder and officially adopted for the Martini-Henry. The most significant change was the density of powder, from 1.55 to 1.745. It still used dogwood charcoal, and kept the same grain size as the older R.F.G., and was still made at Waltham Abbey by the same basic process. But the change in density made the Martini-Henry rifle practical, and the Martini-Henry rifle went on to become perhaps *the* iconic rifle of the Victorian era.

Being able to customize the density of gunpowder is another reason I make my own. In the United States in 2021, there are only two or three commercial options for black powder: GOEX (which may no longer be available at the time of writing), Schuetzen, and Swiss. The consumer of commercially-made black powder has no choice but to use the powder as it is made, at the density it comes from the factory. A density of 1.7 grams per cubic centimeter has become the industry standard for black powder, and all of those brass powder measures sold at every gun shop and from every online shooters supply website measure black powder by volume based on the assumption that the powder being measured will have the standard density of 1.7 grams per cubic centimeter. The practical consequence of this industry standard is that every shooter of every conceivable type of black powder arm – cap and ball revolvers, smoothbore muskets and shotguns, cowboy action lever guns, precision long-range black powder cartridge rifles, and everything in between – is forced to use a "one size fits all" density of powder. The only variables left to the shooter's control is the grain size and brand label on the can.

The subject of powder density was well understood in the late 19th century. A British source from 1880 expressed the importance of density in broad terms:

> No physical property affects the explosiveness of gunpowder as much as its density. Increase of density can only be given by compressing the meal into a smaller bulk. Other things being equal, increasing the density decreases the initial velocity, and, *vice versa*, a less dense powder gives a higher velocity. This is due to the less dense powder burning more rapidly than that with a dense close texture. If two grains or pieces of powder, of equal size and

shape, but very unequal density, be burnt upon a glass plate, the less dense one will be entirely consumed before the denser one has finished burning.

A difference in density of only 0.05 grams per cubic centimeter could alter the known trajectory of a gun to such an extent that it would miss targets. A six-pound cannonball, fired with a pound of powder that was 0.05g/cc denser than usual, had an initial velocity 50 feet per second lower, and at a range of 750 yards, the ball would impact the earth over 100 feet before the target. Gunpowder produced at Waltham Abbey and other prominent government and commercial powder mills in the second half of the 1800s was pressed to a calculated density, with strictly controlled consistency. This ensured that the bullets and shells fired from the guns followed the trajectory that the sights were calibrated for.

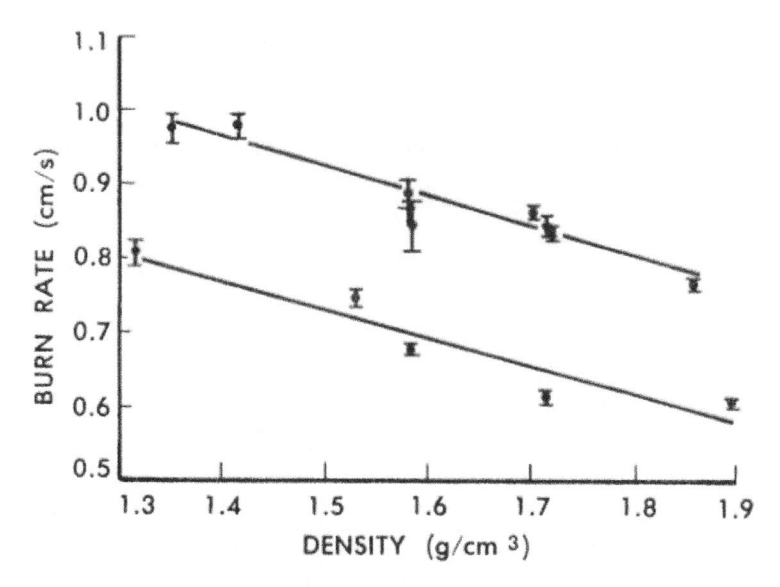

Strand Burn Rates at Atmospheric Pressure as a Function of Density. Lower Curve Oak and Upper Curve Maple Black Powders.

At Waltham Abbey and most other European powder mills, the broken-down mill cake was compressed under considerable pressure by hydraulic or mechanical force

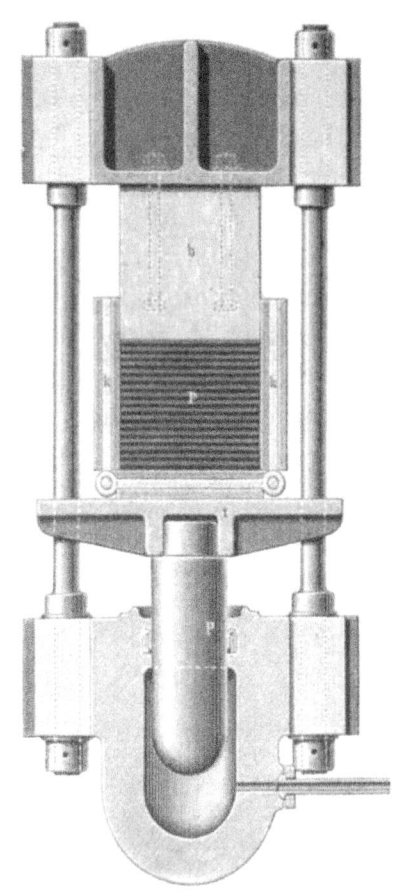

FIG. 96.—One-36th full size.

Section of hydraulic press at Waltham Abbey, showing many layers of gunpowder separated by copper plates being pressed inside the oak-covered hinged press-box.

until it was a dense, solid mass. The "die" of the press was in the form of a hinged wooden box that unfolded when it opened. The box was made out of bronze, lined with oak inside and out. It was actually loaded from the "side," first with a series of bronze plates that had space between them; the broken down mill cake was shoveled in, and it fell down in between the plates until all the spaces were full. Any excess powder was carefully swept away, and the hinged box was then closed back up again, and tipped 90 degrees so that the open end faced up. As many as twenty plates, and twenty layers of powder, were pressed at the same time. A heavy block of wood served as the punch for the die, and as the hydraulic pumps were turned on the plates and powder layers inside the strong hinged box were compressed. Rifle Fine Grain powder was compressed 11.5 inches. A device on the press would ring a bell once the powder had been compressed by the required amount, and the pressure on the press was immediately released. There was no "dwell time" at maximum compression to really speak of; as soon as the powder was compressed to the desired limit, the pressure was lifted and the press opened to remove the powder.

Then the hinged box was opened again, tipped on its side, and the brass plates pulled away from the solid mass of gunpowder between them. The plates had to be knocked loose with wooden mallets, or even pried away with copper chisels. Compression turned the powder into "a hard slate-like cake," that was broken up into pieces about the size of a man's hand. Pressed powder is a curious thing, and when dry, is ceramic hard. Engineering magazine describes powder out of the press as "perfectly smooth and well defined on both sides, resembling so many slabs of black marble, and almost equally hard when dry. It is now collected, put into tubs, and removed to the next magazine, where it is allowed to remain for two or three days; this renders it so hard that it is not easy to break it."

Today, pressing powder is relatively common among serious hobbyists and recreational shooters who make their own black powder. There are even several commercially available black powder press dies available online; a Google search for "black powder puck press" will bring up a few popular options, although they seem to be pretty expensive to me.

I made my powder press dies out of cheap materials. I will not spend too much time on the exact specifics of my press die, because this information is widely available from many other sources, and also because I am in the process of changing my design and anything I describe will soon be an obsolete part of my process. My die is made from a section of 2.5-inch PVC pipe (which may not be the best material for a powder die, due to conductivity of static electricity) that was fitted with a reinforcing band. The pressure would probably shatter regular PVC. My powder is pressed between two cylinders of sand-reinforced fiberglass resin, made to very closely fit inside the pipe, and were cast in 2-inch tall sections of PVC. My first resin discs failed because I used fairly coarse sand; later resin discs made with extremely fine sand have given much better results. I use an ordinary shop press to compress the powder between the resin blocks, and the upper block (the "punch") has been marked to indicate various densities. My shop press is placed behind an improvised barrier of several layers of scrap plywood sheeting; I haven't measured it but it is probably an inch and a half thick. As far as possible, I keep as much of my body behind this barrier while I work the lever on the bottle jack on the press. The angle of the barrier lets me work the lever without any direct exposure. I'm not paranoid or expecting an accident, but if one were to occur, the only damage would be to replaceable property, and not irreplaceable parts of me. Unlike Waltham Abbey, I only press one layer of powder at a time, because the dragon bites.

Using PVC pipe with a round interior diameter as a powder die means that the pressed powder comes out looking like a thinner, flatter hockey puck, and therefore powder pressed in this way is almost universally referred to today as *pucks*. My pucks come out very thin (5.5mm thick) and more resembling a plate than a puck. I press 450 grains (26 grams) of powder at a time. The most time consuming part of the process is weighing out 450 grains of powder, which I put into individual little cups and guard from any wind. My "mill cake" is usually a light, fluffy powder that behaves almost like a liquid, because the particles are ground so finely. It cannot be pressed in this dry, powdery form and needs to be dampened with a very small amount of water, about 3% by weight, which for 450 grains is literally only a few drops. Only a couple drops into the fine powder will cause it to be less of a dust, and more of a powder; this is hard to describe, but it is surprising what a couple drops of water will do. The powder needs to be thoroughly mixed. Too little water is actually preferable to too much; the water will begin to dissolve potassium nitrate and this is absolutely undesirable. Sometimes alcohol is prescribed but I have always mixed my powder with water, as was done at Waltham Abbey. Knowing how much water to add, and how much is too much, is impossible to describe in text, and can only come from experience. A sure sign of using too much water is a white powdery surface on the dried pucks, indicating nitrate that was dissolved out of the mixture and left on the surface of the pressed cake.

A charge of 450 grains is very slightly over one ounce, which means I need to press 16 pucks to produce one pound. However, considering that the next step in the process (granulation) will result in between 20% to 40% in dust or powder fragments too fine for my uses, it really comes out to about 25 pucks for every pound of usable gunpowder in grain sizes that I desire. Measuring out the powder takes the most time, but actually pressing the pucks goes quickly. I used to leave the powder in the press at full pressure for several minutes of dwell time; supposedly, according to internet pseudoscience lore, the sulfur and nitrate partially liquify at this pressure, and form a more cohesive union. While I don't think a long dwell time will harm anything, I don't really think it's necessary and now I will let the press settle at the desired pressure for perhaps thirty seconds, or even less. It goes pretty fast. The pressed pucks are carefully pushed out of the die by hand, and occasionally they stick in the die fiercely. Sometimes I will go out to the press and make a few pucks when I have a spare minute. Over weeks and months, this adds up. I actually have stacks of pucks, some of them pressed four years ago, that have still not been broken down into grains due to the various distractions of life.

Some people with similar black powder dies will press multiple layers of powder, with discs of heavy paper or cardboard or thin plastic sheets in between the layers. In this way, the efficiency of a press can be increased by orders of magnitude, but it also increases (by similar orders of magnitude) the catastrophic consequences of an accident. Explosions in the press houses of gunpowder mills were the source of the greatest damage and loss of life. "Explosions of press houses are by no means uncommon," Captain Smith warns, "and such accidents, if happening when the powder is being subjected to pressure, are the most violent and destructive of all explosions in gunpowder factories." Many amateur pyrotechnicians who make their own powder have argued that pressing powder is perfectly safe, as long as the powder is damp and there are no external sources of heat. History has shown us that this is woefully incorrect, and there is a remote chance (but a chance all the same) that some small pieces of foreign objects, perhaps two little slivers of iron, may contact under pressure and shift in just such a way as to spark. The 19th century presses operated all day, six days a week, and many of them served for 40 years or more without an accident. But others blew up, and killed many people, including an accident in the press house at Waltham Abbey that killed five workers in 1870. So I press one puck at a time.

$$\rho = \frac{m}{\pi \cdot r^2 \cdot h}$$

Because I am making powder intended for use in the Pattern 1853 Enfield, I press my powder to approximately the density of 1.55 grams per cubic centimeter. The equation to determine density of a cylinder is well known, and density equals the *mass* of powder, divided by *pi* multiplied by the radius of the cylinder multiplied by the height of the cylinder. This is easier to calculate in metric. I usually press 450 grains at a time (the *mass,* of 29.13 grams) until the powder cake is slightly over 6mm thick (*height* of the cylinder) in the die, which has a 2.445-inch interior diameter and therefore a radius of 1.2225 inches (*radius* of the cylinder, 31mm). Recently, I have been making my discs of pressed powder even thinner, to be more readily broken up by a roller grinding-mill.

Fig. 1.

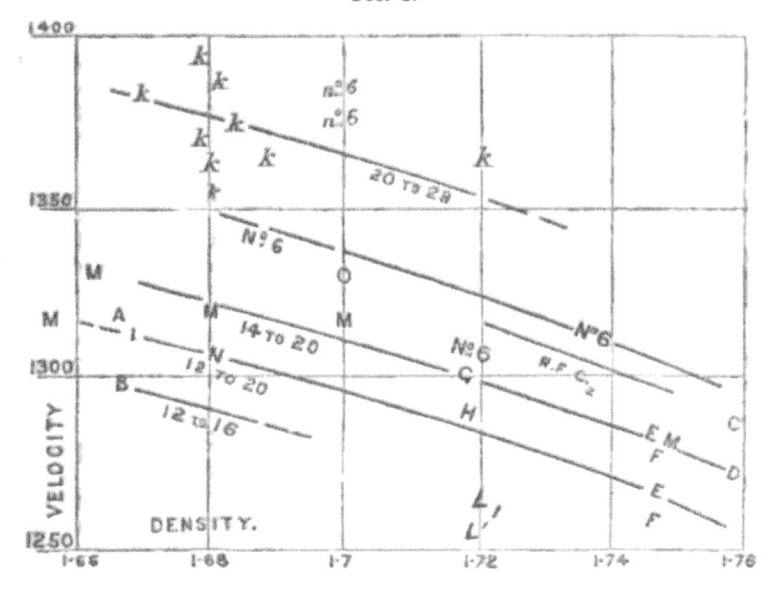

Mark.	Date of manufacture.	Density.	Size of grain.	Date of firing.
A	January, 1870	1·667	14 to 20	January, 1870.
B	,, ,,	1·667	12 to 16	,, ,,
C	,, ,,	1·764	14 to 20	,, ,,
D	,, ,,	1·764	12 to 20	,, ,,
E	,, ,,	1·747	14 to 20	,, ,,
F	,, ,,	1·747	12 to 20	,, ,,
G	February, 1870	1·718	14 to 20	February, ,,
H	,, ,,	1·718	12 to 20	,, ,,
I	,, ,,	1·667	12 to 20	,, ,,
J	,, ,,	1·667	Pass 20	,, ,,
K	,, ,,	1·681	20 to 28	,, ,,
L	,, ,,	1·681	14 to 20	,, ,,
K₁	August, 1870	1·718	20 to 28	August, ,,
L₁	,, ,,	1·718	14 to 20	February, 1871.
L¹	,, ,,	1·718	14 to 17	May, ,,
M	April 21, 1871	1·747	14 to 17	,, ,,
K	June, July, and August, 1870.	1·67	20 to 28	June, July, and August, 1871.
M		1·69	14 to 17	
N	July and August, 1871	1·66	12 to 28	May and August, 1871.
O		1·7	14 to 28	

This graph visually plots the recorded velocities of several experimental powder batches with different densities that were prepared for testing with the Martini-Henry rifle in 1870-1871. Data from these experiments contributed to developing a new powder, designated Q, of higher density and moderate velocity, which was found to be highly accurate with negligible fouling in the .45-caliber Martini-Henry. Q powder was adopted as R.F.G.2 in 1872.

One of the hydraulic presses used at Waltham Abbey.

8
GRANULATION

After being pressed at Waltham Abbey, the hard slate-like fragments of pressed powder the size of a man's hand were allowed to dry for three days, before being taken to the *granulating machine*. This remarkable piece of early 19th century technology was invented by Sir William Congreve, who is perhaps better known for his famous military rockets, in 1819. Even so, they were not actually installed at Waltham Abbey until 1843, when a less efficient and considerably more dangerous form of granulating machine blew up and destroyed itself in a fatal blast. "The granulating machine is very beautifully contrived, and is entirely self-acting, to obviate the necessity of any one being in the building while it is in motion; it consists of a strong gun-metal framework fitted with three pair of teethed gun-metal rollers of different degrees of fineness."

Captain Smith explains that "the granulation is effected by passing the press cake between revolving toothed rollers of gun metal." There were different versions of the machine, some with three pairs of rollers, and by

1870 there were four pairs of rollers. The purpose of the machine was to obtain the maximum possible quantity of the desired grain size, and the least possible quantity of useless dust. The upper rollers had larger and coarser teeth than the lower rollers, which had smaller fine teeth. A conveyor belt brought the press cake up to the top of the machine, and dropped it into the first pair of rollers; from there, the powder slid along a downward-sloping mesh screen, which was also vibrated by machinery to keep the grains moving and encourage those small enough to fall through. If the grains were small enough, they would drop through the mesh screen to more sets of screens below; if too large, the grains slid down to the next pair of rollers, which were tighter and reduced the powder to smaller fragments. Again, if this produced grains small enough they fell down, and larger pieces proceeded to one or two more pairs of rollers, depending on the specific version of the machine.

Grains that fell through the first mesh screen dropped upon a continuous mesh screen below, made of 12-mesh (12 holes per inch). If the grains were small enough to fit through the 12-mesh screen, they fell down to the next continuous screen of 20-mesh. Anything that did not pass through the 20-mesh was the appropriate size for R.F.G. powder, and this was collected in hoppers. Powder that fell through the 20-mesh screen was "dust" and useless for most military purposes; it would be recycled by going back to the incorporating mill, to be broken all the way back down, re-incorporated, turned into mill cake, and then pressed again. Meanwhile, grains that were too large to fit through the 12-mesh screen were brought back to the start, to be run through the machine again.

This elegant and simple machine was completely automatic and ran without any workers in the building. Occasionally they would still blow up, but the granulating machines at Waltham Abbey were well maintained and accidents there were rare. The cause of most accidents were foreign objects that somehow got into the powder and sparked when passing through the rollers. Only twelve hundredweight (1344 pounds, or 610kg) of powder was allowed by Act of Parliament to be granulated at once. The yield in each 12 cwt batch was about 40% in the 12 to 20 mesh range of R.F.G., with the remainder either reduced to "dust" that was fell through the 20-mesh screen, or was still too large to fall through 12-mesh screen. The larger pieces were called *chucks* and they were run through the machine again with the next batch.

Congreve granulation machine, as used at Waltham Abbey.

About half of the gunpowder that went into the granulating house would eventually leave as R.F.G., and most of the dust was sent back to the incorporating mill. Some of the very fine dust powder was retained for filling shells and for use in some descriptions of fuzes (although for various reasons, powder made with pit charcoal was preferred for fuzes, not cylinder retort charcoal).

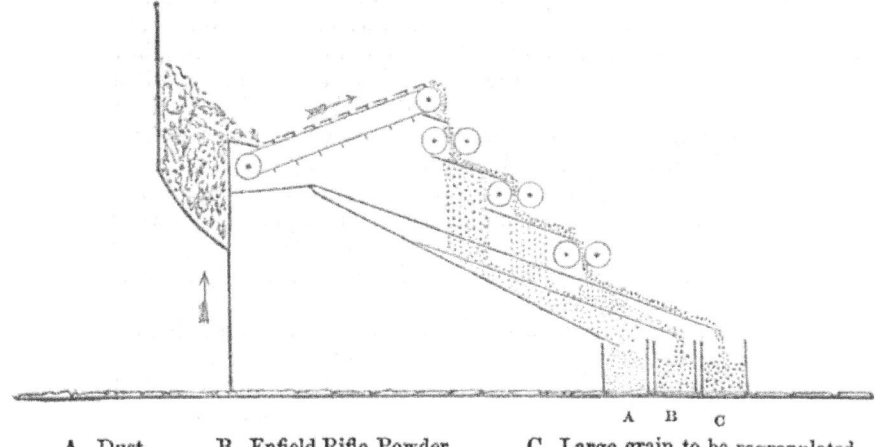

A. Dust. B. Enfield Rifle Powder. C. Large grain to be regranulated.

A cross-section schematic of the granulating machine in use at Waltham Abbey circa 1863. This graphic representation clearly illustrates the various sizes of grain passing through the mesh screens.

After pressing my powder and allowing it to dry for a few days, I am left with thin, hard discs that need to be broken up into grains. This step of the process, while satisfying, is always one of some trepidation. Over these many years I have never had an accident while breaking pucks up into grains, which suggests to me that my methods and precautions are at least generally effective. I always wear a heavy coat, leather gloves, and eye protection during this process, and a full face shield would probably be advisable. When breaking up small batches of powder, should a puck of 450 grains somehow ignite, there would be a flash of heat energy that could cause a significant burn, and any other powder within a certain distance, perhaps several yards, would probably also ignite. Burning black powder is mysteriously remarkable in its powers of propagation over distances. Keeping all of this in mind, I work small batches at a time, taking prudent precautions.

An effective and simple way to break up the discs of pressed powder is simply to crack them into pieces using a heavy implement. Most of the powder that I've made was granulated using just the wooden handle to a sledgehammer, obviously without the sledge. The puck of powder was placed into a plastic bin, that was actually the largest bottom drawer of a cheap 3-drawer plastic shelf. Whatever receptacle is used, it must be absolutely non-sparking and have sides that come high enough to prevent grains from flying out when the pucks are shattered. I put a small rectangle of thin plywood under the plastic bin, and put them both on flat concrete. There is a bit of technique to breaking the pucks up. Simply smashing them with the flat end of the handle will pulverize the powder, and produce dust. Instead of driving *through* the puck with full force, I try to simply *tap* the pucks with just enough force to cause them to fragment. The objective is to break down the powder into smaller fragments of grains, and not totally obliterate it into dust. A couple taps will break the disc up into several smaller pieces, and each of these receive a couple taps, breaking them into even smaller pieces. Once broken down to a point, I pour the contents of the plastic bin through a 12-mesh sieve. Whatever does not pass through the 12-mesh goes back into the plastic bin, to be tapped a few more times with the sledge handle, and so on, until all of the powder goes through the 12-mesh. Then the next puck gets put into the plastic bin, and I start over. I've used different things in place of the sledge handle, but it seems that the size of the head of the handle, hardness of the wood, and degree of control make the sledge handle the best tool that I've found for this purpose.

This method is quite effective. I am able to see into the bin without placing my face or much of my body over it; if the powder was to flash, the only harm would be some blackened soot on my leather work gloves and sleeves of my coat. So far, as already mentioned, I have never had powder ignite while being broken up into grains in this fashion. This doesn't mean that it *cannot* or *will not* ignite.

The disadvantage of the sledge handle & plastic bin method is that it takes quite a bit of time. I have "upgraded" to a new method that uses a pair of teethed rollers to break up the powder discs. Roller grinding mills for breaking up cereal grains like wheat or barley operate on exactly the same principle as Congreve's machine at Waltham Abbey. The material to be ground up is larger than the gap between the rollers, and as the rollers turn, the material is broken down into a smaller size when it is pulled through. The two-roller mill I bought was $65 with free shipping. At its largest setting the rollers on this mill are 0.1-inch apart, and it will not grind pucks that are too thick; this is the reason I press my pucks quite thin. Historically, the Congreve granulating machine was made out of gun-metal, a type of hard bronze once used for making artillery gun barrels. Gun-metal is non-ferrous and doesn't spark. The modern grain-grinding mills are made with food-grade stainless steel, which of course *is* ferrous and *can* spark. I have not yet had an accident with the roller mill, but I do consider it more or less an inevitability. Keeping all the same precautions, if the powder was to flash, the worst harm to result would be sooty gloves and coat sleeves.

The stainless steel rollers on my mill are adjustable, and can be moved closer or farther apart. My powder discs are quite thin, and the rollers are fairly close, but of course, they do not touch and there is no "steel on steel" contact. The particular model of grain mill I have also allows me to connect a power drill to the drive shaft of the rollers, which is an advantage, because it takes a surprising amount of strength to break up the discs. The electric motor brushes of the drill could be a potential ignition source, and I keep this in mind, and take appropriate precautions. I start the rollers turning, and then drop one puck-disc into the gap of the rollers, and quickly withdraw my hand away; the motion is somewhat similar to dropping a shell down a mortar tube. In a couple moments, the disc is pulled through the rollers and reduced to fragments. I place the rollers over a plastic bin (actually the same plastic drawer that I used for breaking discs with the sledge handle), and pour the fragmented powder through 12-mesh. Anything that does not pass through can be poured through the rollers again, or set aside to be tapped into smaller pieces later.

By whatever method the pressed powder discs are broken up, once I have broken them all up and sifted them through a 12-mesh screen, it is ready to be sifted through the 20-mesh screen. I use the stacking sieve set that I probably spent too much for, but they really are supremely useful and by a glorious unexpected coincidence happened to come with two sets of sieves with 12-mesh and 20-mesh. Whatever grains do not pass through the 12-mesh sieve goes back to be broken down further, and whatever passes through the 20-mesh screen is (for my purposes) to be considered "dust." I occasionally save a very small amount of this "dust" powder that won't pass through a 32-mesh screen, to use in cap and ball revolvers, but I shoot very little of that. The desired powder, for my needs, is between 12- and 20-mesh, and for my recreated R.F.G.

The dust (and there is unfortunately always quite a lot) was sent back to the incorporating mill at Waltham Abbey. I usually put the dust back into the ball mill (with hardened lead media) to bust it back down to a fine powder. Then it can be moistened with 3% water and re-pressed, as though it was fresh new powder. At times, when laziness got the better of me, I have put the dust right back into the press with the other slightly moistened fresh powder out of the ball mill, but I was not too impressed with the performance of this powder.

At the end of the granulation process, I am left with a

measure of very rough, sharp, and angular grains of fractured powder, between 12-20 mesh size. At Waltham Abbey, the freshly granulated powder was called the *foul grain*, and was considered unusable in this form. I have used my powder in exactly this form, as it is sifted after being granulated either by sledge handle or roller mill, and it will shoot quite well. However, it does not measure or pour very well, owing to the very sharp and jagged shapes of the grains. It is also covered in dust, and will quickly generate more dust as the fragile sharp jagged bits sticking out from the grains get knocked off. Powder in this state is also exceptionally hygroscopic and will draw moisture from the atmosphere. For the powder to be *durable*, it needs to be processed in a few further steps.

8
DUSTING AND GLAZING

"The granulated powder as it comes from the [granulating] machine contains amongst it a large quantity of dust," Captain Smith explains. "The grain itself is not in a condition to be made much use of as a powder, being rough and porous on the surface and very angular in shape; and moreover the presence of a large quantity of dust amongst it would render it inconvenient to handle and more liable to absorb moisture and deteriorate. A rough unpolished angular grain would also very speedily rub down into dust."

At Waltham Abbey, the *foul grain* was dusted in reels and then "glazed" by tumbling it in barrels. Because R.F.G. powder was made to a lower density, it went through a more delicate processing to prevent the grains from breaking each other down into excessive amounts of dust. A *slope reel*, very similar to that used to sift the charcoal after being crushed, covered in 24-mesh canvas, was used for the *first dusting*, with the R.F.G. powder being run through the reel, which turned at 40 revolutions a minute. "This size of mesh is very large for such a fine powder," Captain Smith cautioned, but it "removes a good deal of the dust."

After the first dusting, the powder was transferred to the *glazing barrel,* which was a very strong oak barrel with an axle through the center, bearing some resemblance to the ball mills used to pulverize the materials. The R.F.G. was tumbled in the glazing barrels for 5 and a half hours, the barrels turning at 34 revolutions a minute. This process polished the grains, knocking away the sharp angles, and rubbing the grains down a rounded shape that would pour and measure much more easily. Glazed powder was given a lowercase *g* after the indicator of grain size, e.g. *FFFg*, to indicate that it has been tumbled and polished, and was therefore well suited for use in small arms. The lowercase *g* does not, as is popularly believed, stand for "graphite." After five and a half hours in the glazing barrel, there was a great deal of dust that now had to be removed.

The powder was then sent to the *second dusting*, which was also done in a slope reel that spun at 40 revolutions, but this time the reel was covered in a somewhat finer 28-mesh canvas. This removed the dust generated by the glazing process.

At this point, at Waltham Abbey the powder was *stoved,* or heated in drying-rooms at 130 degrees Fahrenheit (the heat provided by steam) for at least 18 hours. This drove off all the moisture from the powder, which had been present in the "wet" saltpeter used from the very start of the process, and occasionally supplemented by *liquoring* on the incorporating mill and at the press. The drying-rooms were constructed to circulate the air, so that the moisture coming off the powder was expelled from the room, with no possibility of it being absorbed again by the powder.

Moving the R.F.G. powder to and from the drying-room generated a little more dust, and so it was taken a third time to the *third dusting,* sometimes called *finishing,* this time in a horizontal reel covered in 28-mesh canvas. It was dusted for 2 and a half hours, at 25 revolutions per minute. The gunpowder that came out of the *finishing reel* was "perfectly free from all traces of dust, and therefore fit to be placed in the barrels and issued for use."

Done, at last!

The dusting and glazing processes at Waltham Abbey (and other large powder mills) were designed for relatively large quantities of powder at a time. For example, the glazing barrels each held 400 pounds of powder. My quantities are several hundred times smaller than the batches at Waltham Abbey. For the first dusting, I simply put about 450 grains of powder into the smallest mesh sieve in my stackable set, and shake the sieve gently so that the powder slides over the mesh, allowing the dust to fall onto a large sheet of "butcher block" paper. I usually do this somewhere completely indoors (such as the garage, or a workshed with the doors closed), as any trace of wind will carry the dust away. Some of the dust will be so fine that it will rise off the sieve, and I try to avoid breathing it. This is, of course, highly flammable and I take every precaution to remove any ignition sources. After a time, the amount of dust falling through the sieve tapers off, and when little to no additional dust is falling onto the paper sheet, I consider the first dusting complete. While it is very unlikely that the powder will flash during this process, I still take all the usual precautions with gloves and eye protection.

Glazing can be done in the same ball mill used for grinding down the ingredients and incorporation. No media is used, which substantially reduces (but does not quite eliminate) the possibility of an accident. I don't use the large ball mill that I use for grinding/incorporating the powder, however. Instead I use a much smaller ball mill/rock tumbler of a very common and inexpensive variety, sometimes called a "United Nuclear" 3lb mill after the style popularly sold on that website, although substantially cheaper versions (and probably inferior quality) can be found in the U.S. at Harbor Freight as a "rotary rock tumbler." This small mill/tumbler has a rubberized milling drum and a lid that supposedly can handle three pounds, but in my experience, it struggled to turn a weight of half that. It is adequate for the very small quantities of powder that I will glaze at a time.

Because the rubberized container is not a strong metal chamber, and because I am only glazing a small quantity of powder, I am comfortable enough to tumble batches indoors, in the garage, away from any other flammable materials or sources of heat. One technique, also practiced at Waltham Abbey, to improve the polishing process is to add some larger pieces of gunpowder, about the size of corn kernels, to the smaller grain powder being glazed. I glaze a few ounces at a time, and let the little tumbler run for several hours at low RPM. It should not run at high RPM as this would tend to tear the grains apart; I only want the grains to be slowly polished, rounded, and freed of sharp angles and edges.

After a few hours I remove the powder from the tumbler and sift it through the finest mesh sieve again, as before, to remove the dust. Polishing powder creates some heat through friction, and the heat of the process can cause the powder to "sweat" out a little of its moisture. Being stuck in the rotary drum, the moisture has nowhere to go so it will mix with the dust generated and sometimes will form a thin, hard layer that sticks on the inside of the drum.

The powder still retains a little moisture, but living in a desert climate has some advantages when it comes to drying gunpowder. Scattered out on a tray, left to sit under direct sunlight on a summer day with low relative humidity, will dry the powder as completely and surely as the drying-room at Waltham Abbey. If I lived in a different climate, I am not sure how I would go about drying my powder, except that under no circumstances should the powder ever be dried in an oven at home. If I had a hot water radiator, I would probably build some sort of attachment that replicated on a small scale the steam-heated Waltham Abbey drying-room.

The process of drying will cause a little bit of dust to fall away from the grains so I sift them a third time, and thus finished, the powder is done and ready to be bottled. I save *all* the powder cans that I've bought over the years from GOEX etc., and I prominently label the cans to indicate the type and quantity of powder I have in it, and the date. Mislabeled powder cans are a hazard of sorts on their own, especially when people start putting smokeless powders in them. Because I am an obsessive, I've made custom 19th century style labels for my powder cans with my recreated R.F.G. powder. It adds a certain charm.

A note about graphite glazing: I don't do it, because R.F.G. powder was not graphite glazed at Waltham Abbey. Larger grain powder for artillery *was* graphite glazed, however. By "graphite glazed" I mean that a very small amount of graphite (one half of an ounce of graphite for every 100 pounds of gunpowder) was added to the glazing barrels when the powder was tumbled. This coats the grains in a very thin layer of graphite, and I have to say, it makes the grains shiny and very attractive to look at. Swiss black powder is highly graphite glazed, and it is really beautiful stuff that pours and measures smoothly while bright and shimmering. In the mid-19th century, however, inferior qualities of commercially produced gunpowder were often given a bright graphite coating, to raise the perception that it was a high grade of powder. Graphite is a contaminant, just like the undesirable impurities in the potassium nitrate or the lead from the milling process. Graphite also raises the ignition temperature of gunpowder and makes it harder (and slower) to ignite. For use in artillery pieces, slower ignition was desirable and graphite coating gave the cannon powder this desired property.

Captain Smith acknowledged that graphite coating "gives a fine silvery surface to the grain," but warns that graphite "is really an impurity, and therefore it should be sparingly applied to powder. It is never used with any of the fine small-arm powders, but only with powders intended to be used in large charges, and with the express intention of giving them a surface which will if anything *retard* rather than *quicken* ignition. A great deal of inferior blasting powder is sold nowadays polished with black lead to a high degree of brilliancy, but it is needless to remark that the lustre it possesses is no test of quality." Graphite glazing is sometimes defended as another layer of protection against powder absorbing moisture from the air, which to some extent is probably true, but powder is still hygroscopic with or without a graphite coating and the only real, permanent solution to keeping powder dry is to keep it well sealed against the atmosphere. I have no interest in pretty-looking shiny powder; my interest is strictly in performance, and since Waltham Abbey did not add any graphite to R.F.G., I don't use any graphite either.

In appearance, my R.F.G. is not as dark as commercial powders such as GOEX or Swiss. It is distinctly a lighter gray in color. I'm not sure why my powder is so much lighter, but it is probably because it was not graphite tumbled, and made with charcoal that was not fully carbonized. The smoke is also thinner and of considerably less volume than with commercial powder

9
INTERNAL BALLISTICS

This chapter provides a brief overall survey of the nature and qualities of black powder, and what it does inside a gun barrel. To confess, until somewhat recently, perhaps only 7 or 8 years ago, I knew next to nothing about the actual qualities and properties of black powder, and how it affected my shooting. In fact, I knew *worse* than nothing, because what little I did know was mostly "lore" repeated by word of mouth at the shooting range, around the campfire, and in gun shops. There is a lot of dreadfully bad information on black powder, and how it works, and why we should respect it as a propellant with qualities that no other "black powder substitute" or smokeless propellant has been able to successfully replicate. "A caution must be given as to deduction and generalization in powder experiments," Captain Smith said in 1870. "Nothing is more common than to find hasty conclusions, asserted as universally true." He was careful to "preserve as wide a distinction as possible between what *probably* does and what can be proved *actually* does happen."

We have already discussed the continuous use of black powder in modern-day military applications, because black powder does some things so well that no other substance has yet been found to replace it. Black powder is a *low explosive*, and it does not generate its own shock wave when it goes off. The explosiveness of black powder is a *deflagration*, or an extremely rapid burning, and not an actual *detonation*. The burning or deflagrating of black powder releases energy in such a way, without a shock wave, that it is still used in quarrying and mining operations, especially to recover stones like marble and slate. A shock wave could shatter the stone, while the "softer, gentler" black powder breaks it away in large intact pieces.

We have also already touched on the role of *density* in the burning rate of black powder. Most of the burn qualities of black powder are determined by its density, the size of the grains, and the species of wood used to produce the charcoal (there are other small influences but they are not significant). The denser the powder is, the *more* of the stuff is packed into each grain, and it takes longer for the grain to burn than an equally-sized grain made to a lower density. It is correct to say that higher density powder is truly *slower burning* than lower density powder. A 70-grain charge of FFg powder at 1.745 density will burn slower (take more time from ignition to complete combustion) than a 70-grain charge of FFg powder at 1.55 density. Each charge, however, contains the *same theoretical energy*. There is still the same mass in both, which is 70 grains in this case. The substantial difference is just the amount of time, after ignition, it takes for each charge to finish burning. The faster the powder burns, the more rapidly gases are generated and pressure increases. All of this is given in general terms, assuming all else is equal. There are considerable differences once black powder starts burning in the chamber of a gun, as we will get to shortly.

Even with modern technology, high speed cameras, and precision laboratory instruments, exactly what happens when black powder burns remains something of a mystery. It was the subject of intensive study in the 20th century by Soviet and U.S. military laboratories. Between 1970 and 1990, several major studies were conducted at Aberdeen Proving Ground and while the data obtained was very useful, it was not absolute. A scientific journal article by F. A. Williams in 1976 began with the observation that "although [black powder] has been subjected to scientific scrutiny continually since antiquity, it's burning mechanisms remain poorly understood because of their complexity." That said, we have a pretty good idea and can make reasonable conclusions based on the evidence we have.

TABLE I.—Showing the transformation experienced by Gunpowder after BUNSEN and SCHISCHKOFF.

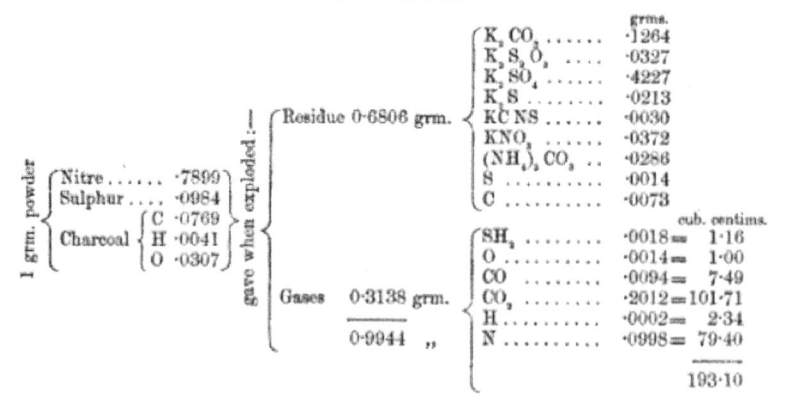

				grms.
1 grm. powder	Nitre ..... ·7899 Sulphur .... ·0984 Charcoal { C ·0769 H ·0041 O ·0307	gave when exploded :—	Residue 0·6806 grm. { K_2CO_3 ..... ·1264 $K_2S_2O_3$ .... ·0327 K_2SO_4 ..... ·4227 K_2S ..... ·0213 KCNS ..... ·0030 KNO_3 ..... ·0372 $(NH_4)_2CO_3$ .. ·0286 S ..... ·0014 C ..... ·0073	
				cub. centims.
			Gases 0·3138 grm. { SH_2 ..... ·0018 = 1·16 O ..... ·0014 = 1·00 CO ..... ·0094 = 7·49 CO_2 ..... ·2012 = 101·71 H ..... ·0002 = 2·34 N ..... ·0998 = 79·40	
			0·9944 „	193·10

Black powder is notoriously inefficient. When it burns, the majority of the products of combustion are solids, not gases. In fact, generally speaking, only about 43% of the substances produced in the chemical reaction of burning black powder are hot, expansive, *propellant* gases. The other 57% are solids, and most of the solids are blown out of the muzzle (see see some of these solids in the form of smoke), but as any black powder shooter knows, an awful lot of the dang stuff remains left behind in the barrel, and this is known as *fouling*. So, for all of the work to make black powder, with pure ingredients, the best charcoal, careful and deliberate mixture and incorporation and pressing to just the right densities, we still only get 43% of what we actually *want* out of it: a hot, expansive gas builds up rapidly at high pressure to drive the bullet down the barrel. As another kick in the teeth, the roughly 57% of solid byproducts (almost 40 grains, assuming a powder charge of 68 grains) get *added* to the weight of the bullet, and the propellant gas formed not only has to push a 530-grain bullet (assuming a P/53 Enfield being fired) but also has to push 40 more grains of worthless crap as well. This increases felt recoil and reduces the useful amount of work the energy of the powder can do.

In all fairness to black powder, it does produce a respectable volume of propellant gas. In laboratory settings, it has been determined that one gram of black powder will produce 280 cubic centimeters of gas. This means a 68-grain charge of powder for the Pattern 1853 Enfield will produce 1241 cubic centimeters of gas. The P/53 Enfield rifle barrel only has a volume of 155 cubic centimeters, so burning black powder generates a volume of gas that is just slightly more than 8 times the volume of the rifle barrel. This calculation, however, assumed black powder is burning at ordinary atmospheric pressure, and standard temperature. There are several physical laws (Charles, Gay-Lussac, Avogadro, Boyle) that describe the behavior of gas in the remarkable environment of a confined metal tube in the presence of intense heat and pressure. For our purposes, we just need to understand that when a gas is heated it continues to expand, and if it cannot expand in volume due to being constrained by the metal tube of the gun barrel, it increases in pressure. Very hot gas (which can reach as much as 2400 degrees Celsius in the chamber of a black powder rifle) will want to expand much more than at room temperature. The exact expansion of hot black powder combustion gases in a gun has not been the subject of scientific inquiry in the 20th and 21st centuries, but several 19th century sources estimate at the gas generated by one gram of black powder would, at maximum temperature, fill a theoretcal space of 2000 cubic centimeters. Therefore, our 68-grain charge of powder would produce a volume of 8,860 cubic centimeters of hot gas, or *57 times* the volume of the Enfield gun barrel. Hot gas, constricted to more than 57 times less than the volume it wants to expand into, is under the relatively enormous pressure of several thousand pounds to the square inch, and this is what pops the bullet out of the barrel at velocities that can exceed the speed of sound.

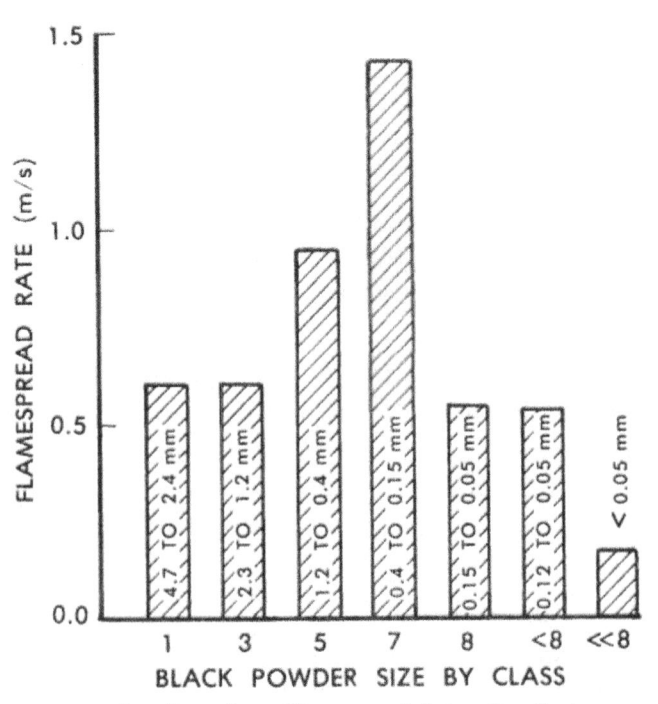

One Atmosphere Flamespread Rates for Various Classes of Black Powder

One of the remarkable qualities of black powder is its *flamespread*. It is important to distinguish and define our terms: the flamespread is the rate at which one particle communicates ignition to the particles next to it, and so on. It is *not* the "burn rate," or *regression*. Burning black powder spreads ignition (flamespread) much, much faster than the rate that black powder actually burns, or regresses. The flamespread of black powder is considerably faster than most smokeless powders, and its ability to spread ignition rapidly is why it remains in use for igniting propellant charges in modern artillery systems. Exactly how the flame is propagated is still not entirely understood, but the prevailing theory is that hot molten salts, propelled by jets of hot gases, are projected from a burning grain and ignite the grains they intercept. In ambient air, the flamespread rate of FFFg powder is between 1 to 1.5 meters per second, or about the speed of a brisk walk. The "powder trails," often poured out of a keg of powder in the old classic Western movies to act as a fuse, is an example of the flamespread of black powder in ambient air. Pretty fast, but not too impressive.

All of that changes when black powder is confined into a closed chamber of a gun. In the open air, the grains are not held in tight confinement physically next to each other; only gravity and atmospheric pressure restrain them, and once ignited, most of the heat and burning particles are emitted into the atmosphere. In the chamber of a gun, the grains are tightly held against each other, and when ignited, the heat, burning particles, and hot gases cannot escape, and the flamespread rate increases by orders of magnitude. In 1976 the flamespread of very large grained cannon powder (larger than Fg) at the fairly low pressure of about 600 pounds per square inch (40 atmospheres) was measured at 66 feet per second (20 meters per second). The flamespread of smaller grained powders has been demonstrated to be considerably faster. Results of a "Flamespread Tester" at Princeton were published in 1980, which produced a pressure of 1450 PSI (100 atmospheres) and a measured rate of flamespread of 328 feet per second (100 meters per second). In mid-19th century firearms, chamber pressures were usually many times higher; the pressure in the chamber of the Model 1861 Springfield .58-caliber rifle musket, for example, has been calculated to be over 6,000 PSI (408 atmospheres). The higher the pressure, the faster the flamespread rate becomes. With chamber pressures *four times higher* in the M1861 Springfield than in the Princeton Research Laboratory's Flamespread Tester, we can reasonably assume that the flamespread in the firearm is even faster.

So what does this mean, practically, for the black powder shooter? It means, in basic laymans terms, that all of the black powder in the chamber of the gun is ignited in a very, very short period of time. It is so fast, that for our unscientific practical purposes, we can almost say it is *instantaneous*. Using the M1861 Springfield, with a charge of 60 grains FFg powder, the length of the powder charge in the chamber is about 0.75-inch. When the gun is fired, from the moment the first particle of powder is ignited by the percussion cap to the very last particle of powder is ignited, is *conservatively* about 1/6000th of one second (the highest published estimate, in research conducted at Aberdeen Proving Ground, put the speed of ignition of an equivalent charge at 1/15,000th of one second). To put this in another perspective, at maximum muzzle velocity, the bullet from the M1861 Springfield moves less than 2 inches in 1/6000th of one second.

Now that all the black powder in the gun is *on fire*, it still takes time to actually *burn* until it is all consumed. Just as the flamespread rate changes dramatically with pressure and temperature, so does the burn rate. In ambient room temperature air, black powder at average density (1.7) burns at a rate of approximately one centimeter per second. Therefore a perfect sphere of black powder, with a radius of one centimeter, would theoretically take one second to burn from the moment of ignition to the last particle of combustible material in the center of the sphere being consumed. At 6,000 PSI in the chamber of a gun, the burn rate is substantially faster.

The *burn rate* is often misunderstood. Technically it is the *regression rate,* which more accurately describes the rate at which a piece of black powder regressively is consumed. A grain is said to burn regressively when it ignites all around its exterior, and gradually burns down towards the center, until it is all burned. Black powder, being a regressive burning substance from the outside-in, ignites rapidly and immediately starts producing a large amount of heat and propellant gas, but as the burning surface area decreases over the course of the burn, and the powder grains burn regressively smaller, the amount of heat and gas produced declines accordingly, until it stops completely. *Regressive burning* is in contrast to *progressive*

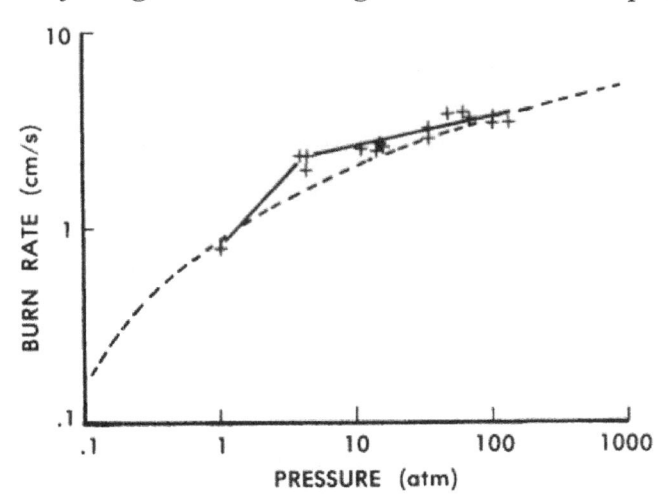

Strand Burn Rates at High Pressures; Dashed Line References 14, 28, 29, and 30.

A graphic representation of the dramatic increase in the burn rate of black powder as pressure increases. From a U.S. Army research paper, 1985.

burning, although the terms are often mixed up. In a progressive burning powder, the surface area actually increases as the burn continues. This is usually accomplished by making grains of powder penetrated by holes. As the holes burn, they get larger, and progressively burn even more powder the longer the burn continues, until it is all consumed.

An example of how fast black powder can burn (and an example of true progressive burning) is the first version of the .303 British rifle cartridge, which used black powder and was fired in the Lee-Metford rifle. Instead of grains of black powder, the Mk I .303 cartridge used a solid black powder pellet weighing 70 grains that completely filled the entire cartridge case (in fact, the case itself was necked down and sized *around* the black powder pellet during manufacture). A single hollow space ran the length of the pellet in the center of the powder; when the primer fired, the powder pellet ignited along the length of this long hollow space, and burned from the center outwards. In the chamber of a .303 rifle, 70 grains of powder produced enormous heat and some of the highest pressures of any black powder military rifle. Accordingly, in this environment of extreme heat and pressure, the black powder only burned even faster, until it was all consumed; the entire pellet was completely burned before the jacketed bullet left the muzzle. Because the black powder ignited along a small hollow space along the length of the pellet, this space grew larger (and exposed more surface area of powder to burn) as the burning progressed, and this is an example of *progressive burning*. Ordinary black powder grains, which are ignited on their exterior and burn inwards towards their center with reducing surface areas, can only burn regressively, not progressively.

With all that said, we can now examine one of the most commonly repeated misconceptions or half-truths about black powder. It's put in many different ways. Some examples of this include: "FFFFg powder is *hotter* than Fg powder," or "FFFg burns faster than Fg." The word *"hotter"* is an American colloquialism most commonly used to describe smokeless powders, where there is a profoundly massive world of difference between truly very slow burning powders, such as those produced for .50-cal BMG, and truly very fast burning powders, such as those made for a .25ACP pistol. It is very inappropriate for describing black powder, however, because the *grain size* of black powder does not change how much *energy* is contained in it. Assuming the powder is the same density, a 70-grain charge of FFFFg contains the same amount of energetic material as a 70-grain charge of Fg. One is not "hotter" than the other. It is exactly the same material. Obviously, the crucial difference is that the 70-grain charge of FFFFg has vastly greater surface area exposed by its enormous number of small grains, while the Fg has a much smaller number of larger grains with far less exposed overall surface area. The FFFFg also doesn't "burn faster," it burns at exactly the same regression rate as the Fg, but because the particles of FFFFg are smaller, they're burnt up in much less time than the Fg. This may be seen as rather subtle, but it is very important.

Captain Smith took pains to explain this concept to mid-Victorian readers in 1870. He probably does a better job explaining it than me:

> Though a charge of powder when fired explodes apparently instantaneously, the combustion is gradual, and the flame is communicated from one grain to another, each grain burning in concentric layers till it is consumed, until the whole is burnt. There is no doubt that equal charges of different [grain size] powders take different times to burn. Two grains of equal size, similar shape, but unequal density, will take different times to burn. In like

manner, the *same quantity* of powder meal, if made into two grains of *very different shape* though of *equal density,* will take different times to burn. When a grain of powder is ignited it takes fire over all the surface and continues burning towards the center in concentric layers till it is entirely consumed. The larger, therefore, the surface exposed the speedier will be the combustion of the grain of powder. A large grain of powder takes longer time to burn than a smaller one, there being, of course, a larger quantity of material to be consumed. If other things therefore are equal, a charge made up of large grains of powder may be expected to take a longer time to burn than one made up of smaller ones.

Put a slightly different way, in the barrel of a gun, a charge of finer grain powder releases all of its available energy in less time than an equal weight of larger grain powder. R.F.G. powder, of 12-20 mesh, would today be considered a very large grain or Fg powder. Colloquial wisdom among the majority of black powder shooters in the United States (I cannot speak for Canada/UK or elsewhere) is that Fg powder "is too slow" for rifles like the .577-caliber P/53 Enfield. In fact, Fg powder is often dismissed as "cannon powder." Why, then, did the British Government go to such lengths to develop R.F.G. (first known as E.R. or *Enfield Rifle* powder) in 1859, with its grain size that today is considered "very large," if it was indeed so unsuitable?

For *muzzleloading* and some breechloading rifles, using expanding bullets, larger grain powder was seen as desirable, in order to reduce the effects of felt recoil and prevent the phenomenon known as "stripping." Expanding bullets, like the Minie (Burton) style and the various permutations of the Enfield's Pritchett bullets, depend on the force of the explosion of the powder and sudden high pressure to physically deform them, compressing the bullets along their length (known as upsetting, or "bumping up" in the U.S.) and expanding them outwards until they completely filled up the windage and formed a tight fit in the bore. Large grain powder was retained in the breechloading .577 Snider-Enfield, which also used an expanding bullet that was sized well below bore size, and even the .577/450 Martini-Henry. In a long, slow-twist rifle barrel, there is no advantage gained by a charge of very fine-grained powder (say FFFg for instance) that would ignite and burn in a shorter amount of time than a large grained powder. The finer powder would release its energy much sooner, creating an excessively (though probably not dangerously) high pressure behind the bullet. In this confined space, the greater surface area of powder burning creates a large volume of hot gas in a short space of time, and as more of it burns and temperature increases, the gas desires to expand even more, creating more pressure. It would *definitely* cause the bullet to upset and expand, but it would also run the risk of starting the sudden movement of the bullet so quickly and so violently that it fails to follow the slow curve of the rifling. Instead, the bullet is apt to head *straight* down the barrel, ignoring the rifling, and this is known as the bullet stripping over the rifling. It was well known in the 19th century, and considerable effort went into finding ways to prevent it. Also, the felt recoil of a 68-grain charge of very fine grain powder in a P/53 Enfield, driving a 530 grain bullet, would be truly brutal.

Larger grain powder, such as 12-20 mesh R.F.G., still ignited almost instantaneously, thanks to the flamespread qualities of the powder. It was also less dense, and so while the grains were larger without very much surface area, the powder itself did truly burn a little faster. R.F.G. powder had no trouble generating sufficient chamber pressure to drive the wooden (or clay) plug in the base of the .568 or .550 inch bullet used in British military ammunition after 1859, and expand the bullet to obturate the barrel. The pressure was not excessive, however, and the bullet was able to overcome its own inertia and begin moving more gradually. It still was *expanded*, filling into the rifling grooves, but it was moving forward while the R.F.G. was still burning. The heat and pressure increased more slowly in the barrel with the R.F.G. than compared to a charge of FFFg, and while the R.F.G. was still capable of driving the P/53 bullet to a velocity of 1265 feet per second (which was *very* respectable in 1859), recoil was surprisingly modest. This was important, considering the somewhat smaller stature of soldiers born in the 1840s, who also had to be taught to aim without flinching or anticipating a punishing recoil.

When using commercial powder, I use 1.5Fg as a sort of compromise between the much less dense R.F.G. (which would have truly burned or regressed faster than more dense commercial powder), the slightly smaller size of the 1.5Fg grains when compared to Fg helping to approximate the actual effect of R.F.G. to an extent.

But whether the grains are large or small, as long as they are equal in all other respects, one measure of a mass of very fine grain black powder contains exactly the same amount of energy as the same measure of a mass of very large grain black powder. As long as all the powder is completely burned up inside the barrel before the bullet leaves the muzzle, an equivalent amount of energy is released to drive the bullet. So whether it is 70 grains of FFFFg or 70 grains of Fg, neither one contains any more energetic material; they both have exactly the same amount of potassium nitrate, charcoal, and sulfur. It is *the same stuff*. There are some applications where a very fine grain powder is desirable in order to release the full amount of stored energy in the powder in as short a span of time as possible. These applications are usually in weapons with very short barrels where there simply isn't a lot of time before the bullet pops out of the muzzle, or in the priming pans of flintlocks where the fine grain of FFFFg priming powder will rapidly communicate fire to the charge in the barrel.

Historically, large grain powder like R.F.G. was also used because of *military necessity*. The British Army, in 1859, was fully expecting the "next war" to be fought at long range. Experiences in the Crimean War (1854-1856), especially at the Siege of Sevastopol, seemed to confirm that trained soldiers, with rifle-muskets, could effectively engage individual targets to about 600 yards, and larger area targets (like infantry formations and even artillery!) out to 900 yards. There were also several celebrated instances of British riflemen silencing Russian field artillery at over 600 yards, at the battles of Balaclava and Inkerman. To propel a bullet out to 900 yards, a fairly stout powder charge was required. In the case of the Pattern 1853 Enfield rifle-musket, it was 68.4 (2.5 drams) of R.F.G. powder. Today we often call this the *service charge*. Everything was very carefully worked out in 1859 so that R.F.G. powder's grain size and density was simultaneously capable of launching a 530-grain bullet out to 900 yards with effective velocity, *and* providing a sufficiently gentle and gradual acceleration of the bullet in the barrel so that it would not strip over the slow-twist rifling grooves.

Personally, I do most of my shooting at what would be called "long range." My P/53 Enfield rifle-musket will clobber a 4-foot square steel target at 600 yards all day long. For this application, the service charge of 68 grains of R.F.G. is exactly what I want and need to achieve the required performance, velocity, and trajectory out of my rifle.

Upon this foundation that we have laid out, now we can discuss the primary reason that I, as a muzzleloader and vintage rifle shooter, appreciate black powder over any substitute or alternative: the effective and rapid obturation and expansion of the bullet. The "pressure curve" of black powder (in any grain size, from Fg to FFFg) is not really much of a curve at all. At the moment of ignition, the flamespread quickly starts the deflagration of the entire powder charge in a very short span of time. This results in a very sharp, near-vertical start to the pressure curve, as the powder ignites and immediately begins regressively burning the grains. Maximum pressure (the top of the curve) is reached very quickly. Then two things happen. First, the bullet begins to move down the barrel, giving more space for the hot high-pressure gas to expand into, and this begins to lower the pressure down from the

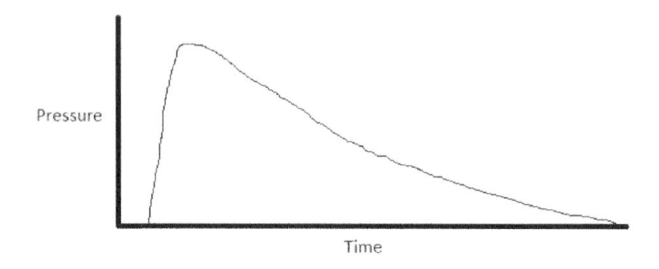

A crude approximate representation of the pressure curve of black powder burning in a rifle-musket barrel. This is roughly the shape of FFg pressure curve; Fg powder would have a slower, rounder curve.

maximum peak. Second, the grains of powder are burning regressively, and becoming smaller as they burn, reducing the amount of surface area of powder burning, which is reducing the amount of gases being generated and also lowering the heat as less powder is burning. The bullet continues moving down the barrel, and as it nears the muzzle, less and less powder is burning; eventually all of the powder is burned, and if the appropriate grain size and density of powder is matched to the firearm, all the powder is consumed before the bullet reaches the muzzle.

What happens to a soft lead bullet during all of this is fascinating. The bullet is an object of considerable mass and density, and using our P/53 Enfield as the representative firearm, this 530-grain chunk of motionless metal is sitting on top of 68 grains of powder. In physics terms, the bullet is an object at rest. Like all objects at rest, it desires to *stay* at rest unless acted upon by a force. The Newtonian physics describing this are far beyond my scientific abilities (my college studies and degree were in history, with a focus on late Medieval religion and the Protestant Reformation, of all things, so please forgive my clumsy layman's explanation). All we need to know is that the bullet is an object at rest, sitting in a hard metal tube, minding its own business, when suddenly it receives a massive hammer-like blow from behind. The pressure curve of black powder, shooting almost straight up like a rocket on the graph, almost instantaneously delivers an enormous amount of pressure upon the base of the bullet. Even before the pressure approaches the maximum, the bullet is being subjected to pressures of at least a couple thousand pounds per square inch.

Imagine, now, a 1-inch cube of pure, soft lead. Place it on a flat concrete surface. Then take a ingot of steel weighing two thousand pounds, and set it onto the small cube of lead. The lead will immediately yield, and squash out, under the massive weight bearing down on it. This is what is happening to the bullet, inside the barrel of the gun. Max pressure inside the M1861 Springfield rifle was estimated in the 19th century to be 6000 pounds per square inch. Some sources put it even higher. In modern firearms terms, this is a laughably low pressure: the German 8mm Mauser cartridge, for instance, produced 43,000 psi). But for that soft lead bullet in a rifle-musket barrel, whether it's 3000 pounds or 6000 pounds or 20,000 pounds per square inch, the bullet cannot resist it. It begins to get squashed, just like the imaginary cube of lead with a one-ton weight pressed down on it.

The physicists also tell us another very important detail:

it takes *less energy* to start to deform and displace a material as soft as pure lead, than it does to overcome the inertia of the material and cause it to start moving. This is almost hard to wrap our minds around, but the soft lead bullet in your rifle-musket barrel starts to get squashed outwards *before* it even starts its motion down the barrel towards the muzzle. Some rifle-musket bullets (like the bullet used in the Pattern 1853 Enfield) used *plugs* as an auxiliary to aid expansion. The plugs were made out of a very hard wood or clay, and had a wedge shape that matched a conical cavity in the bullet base. Because the plugs were very light and had very little inertia, compared to the very heavy lead bullet, the plug also began to move forward before the bullet. It was all of these mysterious forces at work together – the flamespread of the powder, the sharp jolt of the pressure curve, the inertia of the bullet, the action of the plug – that enabled the British Army to successfully adopt a .550-inch bullet for use in a .577-inch rifle bore. Before the .550-inch bullet began to move (or at least, before it moved very far at all), it had been expanded and completely filled the rifle barrel, obturating it, sealing all the propellant gas behind it. Other bullet designs, like the U.S. Burton bullet that is anachronistically called the "Minnie ball" for its external appearance to Claude Minie's somewhat different bullet, hollow out the base of the bullet to allow the 2000+ psi pressure to act not just on a flat base, but inside the hollow cavity, pushing the thin "skirt" of the bullet out, and obturating the bore.

 Even completely solid bullets, with no hollow base or plug, will be affected by the sharp blow of high pressure from black powder, and this will cause such monolithic bullets to also expand. This is known as upsetting, or as bumping-up in common American expression. Bullets that expand outwards to seal the bore are shortened in this process; recovered bullets are often a tenth of an inch shorter than they were before they were fired.

It is possible (and very successfully practiced, in fact) to achieve bullet expansion and obturation while using lighter powder charges than the service charge, and also a finer grain of powder. When this is done, the finer powder (having more surface area) generates a rapid amount of energy in a short time, even though a reduced charge will produce less overall energy than the full service charge, for reasons that by now should be obvious. These reduced charges are able to reliably expand a soft lead bullet, and impart a modest velocity that is capable of some very accurate shooting. Today, probably the overwhelming majority of shooting done with 19th century arms (and reproductions) is with some sort of reduced charge. Alas, I am nearly alone among shooters of black powder military rifles who actually shoots the historic military service charge. Not only is most of the shooting done with reduced charges, it is also done at what would have been considered extremely close range, such as 100 or perhaps sometimes even out to 200 yards. The largest organized shooting group for 19th century black powder arms is the North-South Skirmish Association, which conducts friendly competitions (skirmishes) between various member groups. Almost all of this shooting is done at distances under 200 yards, and the targets are sometimes extremely small and challenging. For this type of application – small targets at close range – the full service charge would be ludicrous overkill, and even less accurate, than a reduced charge.

Over many decades of experience, N-SSA shooters have approached and solved the modern *recreational* challenge of very accurately shooting old military rifle designs at close distances. In the 1850s, the problem and challenge was to find the best powder charge, grain size, and bullet design that wouldn't strip, and would carry the bullet with enough energy to be effective all the way out to 900 yards, with acceptable accuracy at all distances. Today, we no longer shoot these old guns in battle, but for recreation. This posed new problems and challenges: how do we get military guns, designed for shooting out to 900+ yards, shoot accurately at 100 yards?

A premier example of this is my very good friend Rob, from the YouTube channel *Britishmuzzleloaders*, who has achieved great success (and knocked over an unfathomable number of little steel targets) using a reduced, moderate charge of FFFg powder in his Pattern 1853 Enfield. For practical shooting out to about 300 yards, Rob has worked out by trial and error the exact "sweet spot" for his rifle and bullet. For some N-SSA shooters, however, even Rob's reduced charge of 53 grains of FFFg seems excessive and heavy. I know several N-SSA shooters who have turned Enfields and Springfields into "tack-drivers," using specially developed short-range lighter bullets and powder charges as light as 40 grains, or even less! The velocities are very low, and the bullets will drop sharply after about 100 yards, but for the specific application N-SSA shooters require, these loads have been proven to be very successful.

It is remarkable that black powder shooters have achieved so much success in many broad disciplines and pursuits, from 1000-yard precision shooting to 50-yard N-SSA skirmishing, with so few options for commercial black powder. The great accuracy, high velocity, and minimal fouling of late 19th century black powder was the result of the propellant being carefully modified and calibrated to achieve maximum performance in the gun. Today, among commercial powder sources, we have very few options and we are literally forced to take the medieval approach: we have to customize our guns and our loads and our lubricant around the powder we can get. In the 1400s and 1500s, when gunpowder was a poor quality dust and not corned into grains, the primitive guns of the day were built to accommodate the powder. Centuries of refinement and improvement turned this arrangement around, and by the mid-19th century, gunpowder was being customized for the specific caliber and type of firearm it was intended for. Alas, a little over 100 years later, we have almost returned to the Dark Ages because there are only one or two commercial options for black powder, and today we have to customize our shooting around the propellant. We don't really think about it this way, but we have a lot in common with the 15th century gunner building a hooped bombard: both of us can only hope that the powder we've got will work well in our guns.

By making my own gunpowder, I am able to break free from the medieval limitations of having only one or two options, and truly customize my propellant to the application I need it for. Grain size, density, proportions of ingredients, woods used for making charcoal, time and intensity of mixing and incorporation, can *all* be adjusted to produce certain results in performance. As I've already explained at length, making my own powder lets me exploit the enormous amount of research and experimentation that has already been done in the 19th century. I don't *need* to do a lot of trial-and-error experimentation, because I already *know* that the Pattern 1853 Enfield rifle-musket shoots best with a powder of 1.55 density and a grain size of 12-20 mesh that is not graphite coated.

Wahrheitsliebe zeigt sich darin, daß man überall das Gute zu finden und zu schätzen weiß.

Goethe

10
FINAL THOUGHTS

It's somewhat sad and disappointing to consider that we will never have the 19th century's quality of gunpowder again again. All we have are relics, the guns themselves, and the hubris of moderns who assume the 19th century was far more primitive than it was. In rifles like the Pattern 1853 Enfield, it was a perfectly balanced system that matched a customized propellant to the rifled barrel to the projectile. Nothing was taken for granted, nothing just assumed, every piece was the deliberate result of research and experiment that was the product of an emerging industrial and technological science. They did so much more than we give them credit for.

These really are uncertain times for the black powder shooter. As I write this in the fall of 2021, real black powder cannot be bought in the United States for any price. Every online retailer is sold out. GOEX black powder might have been rather uninspiring stuff, made to a military specification fine-tuned for use in fuse trains and artillery propellant igniter charges, but at least it truly was a type of black powder, and readily available. It filled most of the U.S. market share. Now there is a void, and it is keenly felt, and threatens a small but dedicated community of black powder shooters.

So, we have to find and appreciate the good wherever we can. The market may give an elegant answer that we cannot see in the fall of 2021. Some of us may be able to make powder that is every bit the equal (or superior to) the commercial powder that we can no longer easily find.

I have only ever shot real black powder, and I have never pulled the trigger on a load of any type of black powder substitute. You may have noticed the total absence of any mention of black powder substitutes, and that is because I have no experience with them. Due to the fact that black powder substitutes have had their flamespread and burn rates slowed down significantly, in order to meet U.S. Department of Transportation requirements for shipment under a less-strict category of hazardous materials, substitutes generally don't work as well to give that sharp, sudden kick to a soft lead expanding bullet. This means substitutes may not work as well in a muzzleloading rifle. But they're available and fairly cheap, and I certainly will not malign them.

My intent for this book was to increase the appreciation of black powder shooters for our propellant of choice, and to also increase the appreciation for *really good* powder as it was made at Waltham Abbey in the late 1800s. Please forgive me if I have been too technical in my descriptions, or not specific enough; trying to find the balance between an easy-reading survey book and a treatise on technology can be challenging. I sincerely hope this has been useful to you, and look forward to happier times, where the mischievous discovery is plentiful, and abundant clouds of white smoke will roll again over our shooting-ranges.

ABOUT THE AUTHOR

Brett Gibbons is an Ordnance officer in the U.S. Army, historical researcher, instructor, and author of several books on 19th century arms, tactics, and ammunition, including *The Destroying Angel* and *The English Cartridge*. Visit his website at www.papercartridges.com

Made in the USA
Monee, IL
14 October 2022